Aleksandr Konstantinovich
Sokolenko

KEEP

FOREVER

D1444683

Gulag Memoirs
Translated from Russian by Alex Lane

Aleksandr Konstantinovich Sokolenko
KEEP FOREVER (Gulag Memoirs)

Language: English
Translated from Russian by Alex Lane

Maria Feht © 2012
Cover photo: "Kazakhstan" by Dimitri Sokolenko © 2008

Printed in the United States of America by CreateSpace and Feht, Inc.

ISBN-13:   978-1475246896
ISBN-10:   1475246897

Being of sound mind and strong memory, I have frankly and sincerely written down my testimony without the incentive of torture, sleep deprivation, or hunger — as was done to me a quarter of a century ago — to instruct my grandchildren and their descendants.

And just as my trumped up 1944 case file carries the notation "KEEP FOREVER," I, too, bequeath my testimony — TO BE KEPT FOREVER!

A. K. Sokolenko
January 1970

Encounter on the Island of Tears

*In memoriam Ilya Yemelyanovich Semyonov,
on the 100th anniversary of his birth*

KEEP FOREVER

1. In quarantine

Since none of the camp "horsetraders" that had arrived in jail had claimed me owing to my poor physical condition, the camp authorities sent me to the Island of Tears, the lower colony for invalids. That's where they sent the "rejects," the ones who weren't useful for anything at all. It was a transfer point to the graveyard. Though I was still relatively healthy and young (38 years of age), my condition had deteriorated to that of an invalid over the course of several months of incarceration. I lost much strength during a two-month trek from the Don via Moscow, Tashkent, and Semipalatinsk. Night interrogations and torture did their destructive work on me after that. When I reached the common prison, I was half dead. This is what the Island of Tears is about. This is where they send the hopeless cripples from the Patriotic War[1], those who can no longer work due to the excessive diligence of investigative authorities, or just those who are invalids.

While in jail, everyone arrested for a term can't wait to be sent to some colony. After all, there you can at least breathe some fresh air and see the sky. There are more people to talk to there, as well, and work that can help distract your troubled thoughts.

But a convict isn't immediately put in the common zone. First, they've got to keep him in quarantine for two

---

[1] The Soviet name for what, in Western countries, is called the "Second World War."

weeks so that, God forbid, he doesn't bring some ailment into the camp from the internal or common prison.

The quarantine is an ordinary unheated shed with a two-panel door, with small oblong barred windows, and plank beds for fifty people. This shed is enclosed in barbed wire with a gate that is locked each night. At night, the shed was also locked shut.

January. A Siberian frost. Fifty of us are being held in quarantine. After the quarantine, we'll be scattered among the barracks and be immediately sent to work. But now, they're feeding us just like we're freeloaders. Among these fifty convicts there are many who fought in the war that's still going on. They're wearing overcoats. There are a lot of collective farmers. There's two blind accordion players who publicly sang a ditty about the "brilliant leader" with musical accompaniment. In general, they're all laboring people and all of them find themselves in this "rest home" for the first time. It's very cold in quarantine. During the day, everyone's on their feet, trying to get warm. At night, people would spread some outer clothes underneath themselves, and cover themselves with the other part. All fifty people would settle in like herring in a barrel, tightly nuzzled next to each other, and someone among them would cover the rest with clothing. It was a lot warmer to sleep in such a position than by yourself.

I would typically find room in the middle of the plank beds, as I would relate some story until night. Even now, I have no idea where the adventures of my heroes came from. But these were improvisations, and each time, they would end with the words "to be continued tomorrow night."

Despite the terrible frosts, the fifty people in quarantine survive in this cold; not one has croaked yet. Of the previous party, the old-timers told us, half of them got hauled off to the cemetery. They couldn't take it. Unconscientious is what it was. Instead of bringing benefit to the Master, they hastily abandoned their beloved Homeland.

Some among us would receive food packages as relatives found their loved ones. And from these recipients, things would circulate to others, especially to the night-time storyteller. Who will bring him anything? His family is several thousand kilometers away; there are no relatives here.

2. A sudden turn

Ours was a mixed colony. We made furniture and buckets, we sewed clothing, spun, knitted, and wove, we gardened, and there was a subsidiary farm somewhere around fifty kilometers from us, where they grew grain. I wanted to work in my specialty, as an agronomist. During the day, I tried to find out, through the barbed wire, if there were agronomists at the camp, and who they were and how many. To my horror, I learned that there were already three of them working on a small piece of cultivated land, and they were all contract employees. I conclude that I won't be able to work in my specialty here, but nevertheless, I write a letter to the camp commandant and ask him to assign me to work as an agronomist. During the evening check, I hand it to the jailer.

Having taken our gruel in the evening, we lay down as before, side by side, and I continued my narrative.

Everyone quieted their breathing; they were listening. Someone at the edge lit some tobacco, and soon this home-rolled butt went wandering; you took two drags and passed it on.

Suddenly, from outside, the lock clattered and the door opened. A man walked into the darkness.

"Sokolenko! To the commandant!"

Oh, how I didn't want to leave that warmth! And where was my coat? I couldn't find it now if I organized a search party. I pulled someone's overcoat from the pile of bodies and set off to see The Man.

The warmth in the office building was like a caress. In an office illuminated by a dozen or so electric lamps, a completely bald man named Spichglaz sat behind an oak table. He had an agreeable, gentle face and I later learned he was a senior lieutenant.

My prisoner's file lay before him. He merely made sure that I was the right person, and got to the point.

"Have you seen our greenhouse?" he asked.

I answered that I hadn't, and indeed, how could I have seen it if I've been locked up in quarantine for nearly ten days?

"You'll inspect the greenhouse tomorrow, then. It's inside the zone. In three days, you will write a memorandum report to me, telling me what can be grown there in winter. "

I suggested that there were already three agronomists at the colony, and wouldn't it be better for me to first consult with them? But the commandant, for reasons unknown to me, didn't want them to have anything at all to do with the greenhouse. I understood this, and our agreement came about.

A soldier responded to the commandant's bell. The commandant ordered that Rozenfeld be invited. Soon, the bulk of a man, around 45 years of age, clean-shaven and inordinately fat, wearing the overcoat of a senior sergeant, piled into the room. I learned later he was the chief of the surveillance department. Pointing at me with his eyes, the commandant told Rozenfeld:

"This man will be working as our agronomist. Get him bathed immediately, give him a complete new set of clothes, and find him a bunk in the Stakhanovite[2] barracks.

The senior sergeant took me to his office. The commissary manager, bath attendant, and barber were called. The whole operation involving me didn't take more than 90 minutes, after which the senior sergeant and I set off for the barracks.

3. First meeting with Ilya Yemelyanovich

Barracks were locked up at night at the colony. Despite having erected towers in the corners of a huge square, the grounds of which were bathed with electric floodlights, and having German Shepherds run along the outside of the wire perimeter, they were afraid of escapes.

When the lock was opened, we entered a long hall and set off for a set of doors, behind which a pleasant melody could be heard. There were well-serviced iron bunks in the

---

[2] Miner Aleksey Stakhanov was celebrated as a hero for mining 102 tons of coal in 6 hours. Workers who achieved "Stakhanovite" levels were often granted special allowances.

room, and it was light and very warm. The convicts, who had broken up into small groups, were engaged in all sorts of activities: in one corner, short numbers were being performed with two guitars, two balalaikas, and one mandolin; in another, a pair of convicts played chess while a half dozen others "kibitzed" the game; yet others were already lying down on their bunks and reading, while closer to the door, an old guy with a dark mustache was relating how he had bartered his way through the whole war with salt.

There, near this group with the whiskered storyteller, the senior trusty pointed to an empty bunk. I sat down on it and started to listen:

"Yes, my boys," said the black-browed, bewhiskered man of 40–45 years of age, speaking Russian with a Ukrainian accent, "the German planes really hit our station, and as a result, nothing was left of my house and family. Just one deep hole. I was left a complete orphan. What was I to do? So, I set off on foot for the next station, and after that, I made my way further on trains until I found myself at Manycha. I was at the end of the line, with not even a siding left to travel. What was I to do? Meanwhile, all around, there were whole piles of salt. So, I gathered a couple of bags of the stuff and boarded a train for Central Russia. Two bags of salt equals a bag of pennies. A lucky break. And that's how I spent the whole war," he bragged. I took a dislike to the storyteller.

I made my bed, sat down on the bunk, and started to think about the fellows I had left behind in quarantine. How it is that common misfortune brings people together! I'm warm now. But what about them? And who will entertain them in that cold enclosure? The most dreadful thing about being in prison is loneliness. Not solitary confinement, but specifically loneliness, when you have nobody to talk with, even when there are people around. In company, as they say, death itself is beautiful. Apparently, this is not true in any company but only among those who understand you and commiserate with you. In my thoughts, I was back in the quarantine, pressed from the front and back by warm bodies that lay in the dark, covered with clothing.

I was awakened from my thoughts by the approach of a short old man, shaven, with a small gray mustache, carrying a crooked staff. He asked me:

"So we'll be neighbors, eh?"

He set his stick at the head of his bed, than looked at me attentively and asked:

"So you and I, I take it, are here for offenses under the same statute?"

"I'm here under article 58," I replied. "You too?"

"I'm doing my second term," answered my neighbor, and then held out his hand and introduced himself.

"Ilya Yemelyanovich Semyonov, my own parents' son."

Then he asked who I was and what I do. I told him that I had been a college teacher, and that my family was currently living in the Don region. I told him about my trial, my sentence, and of the hardships I had endured over the past few months, starting with the convoy, and then of my confinement at an internal prison[3], and in the common prison. I also told him of my recent meeting with the

---

[3] A high-security prison for segregating persons who have been detained.

colony commandant, and that the camp greenhouse appeared to be my future.

An experienced prisoner, he told me that the worst was behind me, that now I needed to improve my health, that professional people were needed everywhere, and that they were valued here as well. He told me that despite his age, he was working voluntarily as the foreman of a carpenter's shop. "I can't survive without work," he finished.

Turning away to go to sleep, we said good night to each other. As I fell asleep, I felt that now, on my right, was the person I could trust the most on this side of the wire.

4. I am sick

In the morning, after breakfast, I went first to the quarantine. I told my comrades what had happened to me and exchanged the overcoat for my demi-season coat. Then I inspected the GGBU (greenhouse-and-growing-bed unit). The greenhouse was in a derelict state. Many of the window panes were broken, the stoves were dilapidated, and there was frozen earth and snow inside.

On the third day, I brought the commandant an entire dissertation that included estimates of what it would take to repair the greenhouse and the necessary quantity of firewood. I was afraid to pursue the cultivation of cucumbers, and so decided to raise greens (scallions).

My treatise was approved by the commandant, and I set about implementing my recommendations. To help me with the greenhouse, I took on almost everyone who had been with me in quarantine. Some of them, the most healthy, felled trees in the forest and sawed them while others brought the wood to the greenhouse, another group split the logs, while yet another dealt with the soil in the beds. By the first of February, all of the beds were densely planted, one next to the other, with onion seedlings. By that time, it became warm in the greenhouse, and the plant blades began to grow quickly.

Senior agronomist Kruglova did not express any particular glee, as the GGBU had stood idle until I arrived at the colony; but now… This did not reflect well on her. And she was a contract employee, she was getting paid. The commandant, though, was delighted. During one of many visits to the greenhouse, when the green growth pleased the eye, he suddenly announced,

"See here, nobody's to take a single blade from the greenhouse. Chase everyone out of here. I'll be the only one to dispose of the crop."

I asked him to inform his subordinates of his exclusive right to enter the greenhouse. He promised he would do so. And this spared me every kind of uninvited guest.

The first green produce was prepared for the secretary of the city soviet, on whom depended the adoption of some decision that favored the colony Afterward, the produce was increasingly directed toward the managers of Party institutions.

Every day, I related my affairs to my dear neighbor, Ilya Yemelyanovich, and he took delight in my successes. He was particularly gladdened by the fact that colony authorities had petitioned the republican Ministry of Internal Affairs for a work release for me.

But I overloaded myself. While my mind worked perfectly well, I was very weak physically. All my teeth were loose, my gums oozed blood, and my body was covered with small red dots, all symptoms of scurvy. I began to be short of breath, and my heart pounded. I understood that I had become sick.

Once, the colony's chief cook dropped in at the greenhouse.

"You know," he complained, "without greens, I can't eat meat. It's a downright calamity."

"And I've a calamity without meat," I answered him.

In the end, we came to an agreement: I'd give him some of mine and he'd give me some of his. By spring, my scurvy was gone, and I began to look like a regular fellow.

5. "Amnesty"

A hardened criminal about to commit a crime knows what awaits him if he gets caught, and having been sentenced, serves his sentence without complaint (if there's no opportunity to escape). But a person who has committed no crime broods over his punishment and perpetually waits for higher-ups to figure things out so that he, finally, can be set free. And when such "criminals" become a majority behind bars, then a general hope for amnesty or pardon makes its appearance.

About 70 percent of the convicts were serving a sentence for stealing so-called "socialist property." The collective farm workers toiled day and night, and if they had punctually observed the letter of the law, they should have physically disappeared, since they had for years officially received practically nothing for their labors. What kept them alive were their household plots and the fact that they could carry off, often in their pockets, something of what they were producing in common. They would end up in jail in two ways: if they were caught with "stolen goods" or if they expressed their displeasure at the depredations to which they were subject. In the first case, they were tried as criminals for theft of socialist property; in the second, as political criminals. However it happened, they believed that some kind of deplorable error had occurred, and awaited their release. A terrible war was being fought, and it seemed to most convicts that all of the iniquity being visited on them was a consequence of the war. After all, chips fly when you're chopping down trees. So once the war is over and everything's back on track, there'll be an amnesty, and we'll all be home. The entire community was seized by this naive faith. The hope of the convicts for a speedy release was sustained, deliberately, from the outside, and often through very credible people.

Many believed in this forgiving act from above; only Ilya Yemelyanovich didn't believe in it, although he had already once been freed in a special amnesty as a participant in the construction of the White Sea–Baltic Canal, and had been written off a second time because of his age.

He had the following to say about talk of amnesty:

"They chatter like small children. How can these people not understand that there are millions of a versatile work force behind wire? After all, good or bad, everyone busts his gut. Even our group of invalids, they also produce work. As soon as the government decides what to build, they immediately send prisoners there. It's not the same as with contractors, who get asked if they want to go there, and who need to be provided with an apartment and a salary."

Later, after more thought, he added:

"Maybe there'll be one. You see, Stalin greatly rewards thieves. But the political prisoners and the 'embezzlers,' they shouldn't waste time waiting."

It was as if Ilya Yemelyanovich had foreseen the future, because, once the war ended, it was the thieves and — contrary to logic — the deserters who were freed. The war with Japan was still going on, and apparently, the army needed replenishment. But the war ended soon, after the Americans dropped atomic bombs on Japan. As a result of the victory, the thieves and deserters obtained their complete freedom.

Ilya Yemelyanovich used to tell how, as an active participant in the construction of the White Sea–Baltic Canal, he had been freed in a special amnesty as a result of an administrative petition. I asked him to tell how he was later written off on account of his age.

"Well, it was just before the war started," he said. "A lot of us old geezers were assembled on this island, and the government started to incur losses on our account. So they convened a commission, executed the papers, and soon showed us the gate. They wrote the whole lot of us off, regardless of the article that landed us here.

And it turned out that at that time, I was building a cart for the commandant. So the commandant calls for me and says,

'Listen, Ilya Yemelyanovich, I'm asking you to please finish the cart for me, and then you'll go home, and not with empty hands.'

So I thought about it and agreed. And while I was finishing the cart, the war began. Everyone who'd been convicted under article fifty-eight was ordered held back. I got held back as well. And so, as you see, I'm still here, waiting."

He fell silent and thought for a while, then looked at me and finished what he had to say.

"But as far as living out your last years is concerned, it's six of one and half a dozen of another. At least here, you know they can't arrest you!"

6. Merchant

The foremen in the furniture shop that was run by Ilya Yemelyanovich used to say he had golden hands. First, he was a wonderful machinist, smith, saddler, and shoemaker. He put love and a lot of knowledge into everything he made, and put his soul into everything he did.

Once, before the war, the colony participated in some kind of exhibition of industrial articles. With his own hands, Ilya Yemelyanovich made a saddle for the exhibition. His saddle received the highest mark and then departed for Moscow as the best exhibit item.

He would evaluate the quality of steel by looking at the kind of sparks it generated when pressed to a grinding wheel, and he could then tell if the steel could be used for one article or another.

Ilya Yemelyanovich should have been a scientist. He knew how to get into the heart of what he was dealing with, and if he encountered some kind of ambiguity or riddle, he'd try to figure it out and often succeeded. This man stood with both feet firmly planted on the Earth, loved it, and was very inquisitive. He spoke excellent Kazakh, Chinese, and Mongolian. He had a colossal memory, although he had never attended school. A fugitive soldier taught him how to read, write, and the rudiments of arithmetic.

Once, I asked him to tell me his biography.

"How could somebody like me have a biography?" said Ilya Yemelyanovich to me. "As though I were Volodya" (Ilya Yemelyanovich always referred to Lenin using the diminutive of Lenin's first name and explained that "We were born the same year").

His grandfather, a hero of the Patriotic War of 1812, had been with our troops in Western Europe, had a good look at how people lived there, had no desire to again go under a landowner's yoke and skipped across to the free lands in Siberia, ending up in Altay and settling down on unowned land near the Katun River. There, he found other fugitive Russians who had settled down in this land of riches and fabulous marvels, the Russian Eldorado. He built a water mill on the Syoma River, started a bee-garden, trapped animals, prospected for gold, and did some blacksmithing.

Ilya Yemelyanovich's father, Yemelyan Semyonov, was a man who could barely sign his name but had a colossal memory. He dealt in livestock and was hardly ever at home, traveling often along the trade routes of Siberia,

Kazakhstan, China, and Mongolia with his large herds of cattle and flocks of sheep. He kept no accounting books. He kept all of his business affairs in his memory. By the way, Yemelyan Semyonov had no capital of his own to fund his commercial operations. He had ties with guild merchants in Moscow, and obtained his credit from them.

In 1900, after Holy Protection[4] Ilya Yemelyanovich's father suddenly died after having returned from Moscow (to where he always traveled at that time of year to settle debts with his creditors).

After burying his father, Ilya Yemelyanovich became lost in thought: What should he do? He had learned many trades from his grandfather (who had died long before). He had traveled many thousands of *versts*[5] over trade routes, too, helping his father. Ilya Yemelyanovich decided to travel to Moscow, to his father's former boss. He traveled to Omsk on horseback, and then on to Moscow by railroad train. The Moscow boss had never seen Ilya Yemelyanovich in the flesh. Upon meeting him, he looked at him sharply and asked:

"You couldn't be any other than Yemelyan's son." Sensing bad news, he added, "So what happened to your dad?"

"Yes, I'm the son," confirmed Ilya Yemelyanovich, "and I recently buried my dad."

The merchant invited him to his house and questioned him for a long time about this misfortune. A merchant's

---

[4] A reference to the feast of the Intercession of the Virgin Mary, celebrated on October 1 (Old Style) / 14 (New Style).

[5] A Russian *versta* is a unit of length equal to 1.067 kilometer.

business is dangerous. A merchant always has money about him, and many people hunt after money. Wherever you might be, whoever you meet, always be on guard, or they'll quickly dispatch you into the next life. Learning that Yemelyan had not been the victim of highwaymen, the merchant became somewhat calmer and finally asked,

"So, what are you thinking of doing? You, apparently, also want to be a merchant?

"Yes I do, like my dad. I've traveled quite a bit over his trade routes. It's just that I'll need a little money."

"For money, come by tomorrow. There's money."

"The next day," related Ilya Yemelyanovich, "the merchant and I met face to face and he handed me forty thousand in bills, without any documents or receipts, and we parted."

7. Qamulaqs

Before the First World War, Ilya Yemelyanovich was constantly moving along the trade routes between Russia, China, and Mongolia. Wherever he was, whomever he met with, he was everywhere a welcome guest. With an excellent command of many Asian languages, he was well familiar with the daily life, customs, proverbs, sayings, and stories of the people with whom he dealt.

He knew the thousand-kilometer long trade routes, the grazing lands, and the watering places, he knew how and at what time to arrive at this or that fair, so that his animals would be alive and well with no loss of marketability. He was not only a merchant-proprietor, but also a good livestock specialist and veterinarian. On a tall jumper, with a revolver in his pocket and a rifle behind his back, he would ride fast ahead of, then behind his numerous flocks.

"It was particularly tough for me," he said, "when I was returning from a fair after selling my livestock. I would also buy up all the substandard livestock left over after the other merchants had sold their stock at the fair, so that if I would arrive at the fair with, say, fifteen thousand animals, I would often take away almost as many. Let me tell you, it took a lot of effort and skill to turn these "rejects" into sellable livestock for the next fair!"

"Pardon me, Ilya Yemelyanovich," I interrupted, "but do you know that now, you merchants are being called exploiters, bloodsuckers, and the ruin of the peasantry? That when talk turns to merchants, that some kind of great debauchers and arch-devils are called to mind? And you speak of labor?"

"Oh, those are windbags who have never seen anything not in their books. A merchant's labor is difficult and dangerous. You're not the only one on the market; you've got a lot of competitors. Each offers his own price to the peasant, who is also not stupid, and who selects the most advantageous deal. For this reason, it's not as if you'll get too much off him. And then, that peasant, for whom so many now shed their tears, only got rich on the money he got from merchants, because he now had the opportunity to develop his own production for the market."

Then Ilya Yemelyanovich waved his hand in disgust and finished what he was saying:

"A merchant had no time to get drunk or behave in an improper manner. And if it did happen, it was after he had completed some difficult task. Generally speaking, Russian people like to let loose after work. Why is a merchant any different? Let me tell you of a time when I let myself unwind and get involved in something that was a sort of game and not business.

I was coming back from a fair in Irkutsk with fifteen thousand head of sheep. That's fifteen flocks. I left the town with these infirm animals that I had bought for a song. Happily, the weather remained good, and so did the grazing land. Over a couple of months, you wouldn't have recognized my cripples: no ailments, no die-off, in fact, they had become fatter. It brought joy to my soul. I noticed how, on the road, about fifteen Kazakhs went by on horseback. The next day, I see that the same Kazakhs had returned.

They asked me if I had seen a young Kazakh woman. It turned out that the youngest wife of the old *bey*[6] had run off. I was still young myself, and things were going well. And so I developed an interest in this Kazakh girl. In those days, my eyesight was as sharp as an eagle's!

So this one time I'm riding my jumper in front of my flock to a pasture where haystacks were scattered about. I look, and near one stack I see a person. "The Kazakh girl!" I think. I start to call out to her in Kazakh, but she doesn't answer. But nevertheless, I made her start talking, after promising to deliver her to her parents. In the evening, when one of my flocks was passing through this pasture, I hid the young woman in a cart with medicines. Nights, she would come out of the cart, the herdsmen would feed her, and we moved toward where her parents lived. As for me, I went on ahead. I saw that the parents of the Kazakh girl had

---

[6] A title for a local chieftain.

been weeping. They thought that their daughter had been eaten by wolves.

I asked them to give me the *qamulaqs*[7]. The first time I laid them out, I announced to the parents that their daughter was alive; the second time I laid them out, I said she was not far from them; the third time, that she would be home the following morning.

The Kazakhs took heart again. They looked at me as if I was an oracle, seated me at the place of honor, and fed me like a distinguished guest. And when their daughter returned to them in the morning, the father gave me ten sheep as a gift, which I refused.

So that's how I spent three days away from my business as a merchant, involved in this story I just told you about the runaway Kazakh girl. And I could only allow myself this diversion because my affairs were proceeding splendidly at the time.

So there's your mercantile arch-devilment for you," he concluded.

Ilya Yemelyanovich had one other weakness. An international group of performing wrestlers traveled with him in a cart belonging to one of this flocks. In Russian hamlets, Kazakh *auls*, and Mongolian or Chinese villages, Ilya Yemelyanovich would perform with his theater in the language spoken by his many listeners.

His performers were trained marmots, which he caught in the Tyan-Shan mountains when the animals were very young. Through extensive drills, he trained the marmots to

---

[7] Kazakh divining stones.

‚obey his commands and demonstrate marvels of wrestling on an improvised stage.

But Ilya Yemelyanovich occupied himself with his performers only when the mood struck him. And his mood was linked directly to the overall state of his business.

8. Beekeeping

The First World War was being waged. Ilya Yemelyanovich was a member of the peasant class and was drafted into the army. He took up the baton of heroism that had been passed by his grandfather, who had fought in the Patriotic War of 1812 and, in his first year of service, Ilya Yemelyanovich was awarded a pair of crosses for acts of heroism. He had wanted to become a full Knight of St. George, but at the end of 1915 he suffered contusions, landed in a hospital, and after recovering from his wounds, received a full military discharge for health reasons.

"When I returned home," related Ilya Yemelyanovich, "the question popped up anew: What should I do? Good health was needed to be a merchant. So that choice was eliminated on its own account. When I was a child, my grandfather and I worked a lot with bees, so I knew the business, and I was again drawn to it. At the headwaters of the Katun, I found a place that wasn't good for anything except beekeeping and bought it from the community.

The parcel consisted of a hillside that faced south, covered with forest, through which flowed a jolly little stream. First, I felled logs for the future beehives and built a workshop at the stream, with a saw bench and all sorts of mechanical gadgets for sawing, shaping, and other work.

All of these devices were powered by water from the stream.

A year after I started work, there were a thousand hives in my apiary. I sent away for bee colonies from abroad, by mail, through the St. Petersburg beekeeping society. They arrived in packages. There was a lot of work involved, but the business went well. During the season, I sold merchants around thirty-five thousand pounds of honey alone. And that doesn't take account of the beeswax!

A Professor Kozhevnikov[8] in St. Petersburg became interested in my work. Based on his specifications, I managed a substantial amount of experimental work in my apiary. The professor later even wrote a small book about this. It was published. Kozhevnikov himself came from St. Petersburg to visit me at my apiary.

One time this phaeton touring car stopped at my apiary, and a man got out who was not from our parts. Catching sight of me, he asked,

"Is this the apiary of Ilya Yemelyanovich Semyonov?"

"Yes," I answered.

"Would it be possible for me to see him?"

"Go ahead and look," I answer. There's no law against looking.

"But where is he?" asked the perplexed professor.

"Here he is! I'm him!" I reply.

---

[8] The published work of Grigoriy Aleksandrovich Kozhevnikov (1866-1933), on the instincts and evolution of honeybees, is still considered the best in the apicultural literature.

My appearance was not much to look at, and in those days people always took me for Ilya Yemelyanovich's workman.

We became acquainted. He spent a couple of weeks with me and studied my business. He liked everything. Apparently, he liked me, too.

Per the professor's plans, besides everything else, I started a bee stock-breeding program. Although my academic manager lived in St. Petersburg, we corresponded often, and our stock-breeding business went well. Eventually, I managed to successfully cross the Caucasian mountain bee with the local bee. I wrote about it to the professor. I waited and waited, but received no answer. Later, I found out there had been a revolution in St. Petersburg. It took a long time for the news to reach us. Later, the Whites and then the Reds started to appear in our area, and do you know what they had in common? They all loved sweets. At first, they'd come visit, but later they'd act in an intimidating manner, as if I and my bees were spreading counterrevolution. At that point, some bears showed up out of nowhere and started to overrun the apiary. I watched it all, and watched, and one night, I took off, as they say, for parts unknown.

In the end, I found myself among some Mongol friends of mine in Mongolia. I caught a pregnant marmot and waited until she whelped five little marmots: two females and three males. I let the mother and the daughters go in the mountains, and got down to work with the boys, and soon I had the same theater with acrobat wrestlers that I had when I traveled the trade routes. At the same time, I treated livestock that belonged to Mongols, and treated people as well.

9. The White Sea–Baltic Canal[9]

Time passed. My performers turned from youngsters into venerable marmots.

Odd bits of information would come from the motherland, hinting that a peaceful life had come about.

One day, a Soviet livestock importation representative turned up in the village where I lived. He proposed that I start working for him as a livestock procurer in Mongolia. I was acquainted with the business, and soon I was a Soviet trade worker. The work was so easy, it was funny. Now I no longer had to worry about competitors (the territory of Mongolia had been divided among several of us Soviet "merchants"), and after I acquired livestock from the Mongols and passed it on, I no longer worried about its safekeeping. It wasn't the way it was before. Nobody interfered as far as price was concerned, and as I've said, there was no competition. No longer did my head ache the way it did before, about how and to whom the livestock would be sold. The work was so comfortable, that even my belly began to grow, which had never happened before.

Naturally, every year, I'd return to my native country for a visit. I saw how the people had truly and heroically restored their economy from the ashes of the Civil War. My spirit was happy.

---

[9] The infamous White Sea–Baltic Canal (*Belomorsko–Baltiyskiy Kanal*, or *Belomorkanal*) is a ship canal in Russia opened on 2 August 1933. It connects the White Sea with Lake Onega, which is further connected to the Baltic Sea. The canal was constructed by forced labour of Gulag inmates and during its construction some 100,000 people died (although various estimates have been stated).

But then at the start of the 1930s, there began the eradication of what had successfully been created. The numbers of cattle, horses, and sheep began to dwindle catastrophically in our country.

"What's this mean?" I asked the commissars with whom I met.

"Such," they would say, "is the policy of the Party."

I did not remain quiet. How can it be, that everything that our people has lived on since the beginning of time was being eradicated? What kind of policy is this, if swarms of *arat* herdsmen flee to Mongolia and Kazakhs to China, like rats abandoning a sinking ship? Something's not right, here. Someone's inflicting harm. I was immediately invited to confer with the appropriate authorities. 'You,' they said, 'are an accursed anti-Soviet!' 'You,' they said, 'must be soundly reeducated, so that you understand what's what.'

They hung ten years on me and sent me off to the White Sea–Baltic Canal construction project.

I've never been afraid of work. Work is a blessing for a man. What's frightening is jail without work, where you're ready to do harm to yourself. I was still young then; just past 60 years of age. There were thieves there, as well as dignified people, mostly scientists and engineers. A lot of people left their bones there. In my team (I was the team foreman) there were professors, and even one academician. All of them had been sent there, the way I had been, for reeducation. One professor kept explaining about how Peter the Great built Petersburg on the bones of peasants and compared that construction with the construction of the White Sea–Baltic Canal. Like many "academicians," he died there. Later, after barracks had been built, the food got better and many made it through and were sent home before having served their full sentence upon completion of construction. That's how I left Stalin a whole five irredeemable years.

10. Novosibirsk

I showed up at home in Novosibirsk. My son arrived there. My old lady lived with him, too.

Now I had been reeducated. In town, there were long lines for bread. There was no lard and no oil, but I kept my mouth shut. If previously they had been grabbing the small fry, now they had begun to grab the big fish, the commissars with their Orders. I kept my mouth shut. I began working as a machinist at one plant, and people were being grabbed from there. That didn't help with production, of course, but I kept my mouth shut. Then they started to grab the people who hadn't been saying anything, the idea being that "If they're keeping their mouths shut, it's because they're plotting something quietly!"

I got tired of living in barracks, so I decided to build myself a small wood house and quietly live out all these times. I'll plainly state that I'm a pretty good woodcarver. I never went to school for it, but I was self-schooled. So I decided, with my stupid (though reeducated) head, to decorate this little house in the old Russian fashion. What I ended up with wasn't a house but, as one regional ethnographer put it, a "work of art." Tour groups started coming around to look. I was written up in the paper, where I was called a "people's handyman" and a skillful artist.

11. Another ten years

It fact, it turned out I had not been reeducated. And why did I start in with the carving? (I still ask myself that question.) My art caught the attention of other quarters and I was summoned.

"You are Ilya Yemelyanovich Semyonov?"

"Yes," I say, "I'm the son of my own parents."

"So it's you," they say, "who was once convicted and served a term of sentence?" And they haul out my old, familiar file stamped " KEEP FOREVER."

"Yes," I say, "that's me." "But if you please," I say, "for my foremost participation in the construction of Stalin's White Sea–Baltic Canal, I was released before the end of my sentence."

"That fact," they said, "is known to us. But it is of no interest to us. What is of interest is your current personality. We have decided to detain you."

"What do you mean, 'detain'? I'm a worker, I work as a machinist at the plant, and on major holidays I receive commendations from the administration for having exceeded…"

"Yes," the investigator interrupted me, "we are aware of this current tactic of our potential enemies, to perform at even Stakhanovite levels at first, only to drive a knife into the back of the revolution later."

Quite a number of such "enemies of the revolution" were rounded up, and so as to give the verdicts something of a legal aura, a special meeting of the Ministry of Internal Affairs was convened at the Kremlin. This meeting didn't bother to legally substantiate its decision, but simply sentenced this victim or that to a term of punishment: ten years.

Things turned out just as in Krylov's fable[10]: "I want to eat, and that alone makes you guilty!"

12. In the "joiner's shop"

When I topped 70 years of age, they decided to write me off. I've already told you about what happened as a result. Because of my age, I was sent to this very same colony of invalids with the idea that it would be the last place I'd be sent in life. From here, the only place you get sent is the graveyard.

At the colony I began to have the right not to work and receive 550 grams of brown bread and the common gruel. This is what I've worked so hard to achieve. Out in the world, for sure, nobody'll give you a gram without payment, but here, it's:

'Ilya Yemelyanovich! Here's your ration of bread and gruel, if you please.'

But as you know, I can't sit on my hands and not work. The furniture shop is considered the leading department at our colony. It contributes the largest amount to our money box. And so the colony commandant asks me to head up this shop.

"You," he says, "don't do anything. Just sit and watch to make sure things are done right."

---

[10]   A reference to Ivan Krylov's *The Wolf and the Lamb.*

I've never been a drunkard but I make it a rule to have a small glass before dinner. Without it, dinner isn't dinner. So I tell the commandant:

'Okay. I'll agree to work for the benefit of the colony. Only tell your ruffians' — that's what Ilya Yemelyanovich called the jailers — 'to stop confiscating the vodka that people sneak in from the outside for me. I've got to swallow a small one before dinner. That way, the work will also go successfully.'

'He agreed, and it's been already four years that I am setting my carpenters' heads straight. I also got the commandant to agree to a second condition, that nobody disturb me during the night shift, because I really love to get a full night's sleep.

This condition, thank God, is also fulfilled. It's good when work in the shop runs smoothly and everyone knows his place and his business. But here's the bad part: You teach a guy and start relying on him, and suddenly, his sentence is up. You have to train new ones.'

I saw myself how Ilya Yemelyanovich trained the new guys whose arrest files showed that they were, by specialty, carpenters and even joiners. The supervisor of the furniture shop was very strict with them.

"And how did you approach the workbench?" he would suddenly pounce on a new guy with a question, or:

"How are you holding that tool? What are you, some kind of cripple?"

He'd get down from the platform that stood in the center of the shop, from where he could observe how everyone worked, and he'd take the tool from the new guy and show him how to position himself and how to use the tool. And there were times when, during an entire shift, he wouldn't step away from the workbench, but keep working like a craftsman.

It was apparent that whoever learned his craft under Ilya Yemelyanovich's eye became a lifelong first-class joiner.

Ilya Yemelyanovich would be terribly exhausted after each shift. But after a stoup of vodka and a good night's sleep, he was ready to work again.

A lot of his physical efforts were spent on various unplanned side orders for furniture from the large number of higher-ups. Time spent on such projects couldn't be entered in the time sheet for completed work. So all that work was done by the shop supervisor with his own hands, so as not to reduce legitimate production, because the latter defined the amount of the bread ration and miscellaneous supplements. And Ilya Yemelyanovich always fought to make sure the workers in his shop got a fair ration.

"A hungry man is not a worker," Ilya Yemelyanovich would say.

13. Always ready to build coffins

March came to an end. But the cold Siberian frost remained outside. The colony shops were heated, but the barracks weren't (except for those where the "Stakhanovites" lived). People would get terribly cold at night and anxiously awaited the start of their shift, so that they could get warm on the job. After the morning check, a large ox-drawn sledge would be brought up to the barracks, and those who had died during the previous night would be brought out and loaded onto it. The sledge was later taken to the medical unit. A doctor would come out and check the bodies, checking the pulse of some, to make sure no criminal would somehow escape, after which the sledge was hauled off away from the colony. The corpses would be piled up somewhere until the ground thawed, after which they would be buried.

Today, Ilya Yemelyanovich wasn't the one talking and I listening. On the contrary, it was I who was relating an incident. The greenhouse driver had died that day. I had first met him in the quarantine room at the common prison. He was serving a short sentence and was waiting to be sent off to work at a camp. For that reason, he was asking experienced convicts about the conditions of camp life.

"I'm a former miner. I'm not afraid of work," he said. "I'll always earn the very highest bread ration of 950 grams."

And I, who had spent my entire life reading books, now envied the physical strength of my brother-in-captivity. They took him first. Where he went, to what camp, we weren't told. But now, finally, I'm in a camp, too. To my surprise, it was there that I met my miner.

"So, how are things? How's work?" I started to ask him. It turned out that things were going very badly for him. No matter how hard he worked, the foreman wrote down an amount equal to what was left over after crediting all his friends with work completed. It turned out that here, your bread was not earned by labor, but by how well you were liked by your foreman.

To relieve my friend of this injustice, I took him on at the greenhouse as a cart driver.

"A couple of oxen, a sledge, you bring firewood to the greenhouse, take fertilizer away to the field, and every day you'll get 950 grams of bread, along with the common and hospital supplement. Nobody gets any greater amount for any sort of work," I told him. He happily agreed and started to work. But by that time, he had become very weak physically. It was very cold. He spent the day in the cold and slept in a cold barracks at night. In the end, he fell ill and soon died.

So there I was, telling Ilya Yemelyanovich this story. Soon after, despite the late hour, the door to our room opened and the head of one of the jailers appeared. He summoned Ilya Yemelyanovich. This was an extraordinary occurrence, as nobody had ever summoned him at night.

Soon, he returned from the mud room and hurriedly began to dress at the coat rack. Then he came up to me and asked me to hand him, from behind his headboard, the hook-shaped stick that he carried with him everywhere. I gave it to him and asked,

"How is it, Ilya Yemelyanovich, that you're breaking your own rule to never go out on the night shift?"

He bent over and whispered in my ear:

"I'm going to build a coffin. The senior jailer, Moskin, died."

Then, with a smile, he winked at me and added:

"For them, I'm willing to stay up all night long to build coffins." And he left.

14. Chess player

The next day, Ilya Yemelyanovich was in a good mood, apparently on the occasion of jailer Moskin's death. It was even surprising how death could evoke a feeling of satisfaction.

It turned out that Ilya Yemelyanovich had known this Moskin for a long time, and this is what he told me of him. Moskin was a typical parasite, who relentlessly sucked the blood of prisoners. Thin and tall, he was always on the lookout to take something away from a convict. He strained at nothing and hauled all manner of things from the colony to his own home, including food that had been delivered by the relatives of convicts.

He had professional thieves — *urki* — working for him in the camp. They'd steal something and go straightaway to Moskin in the jailer's office. The owner of the article would run around and eventually settle down, but the item would end up at Moskin's apartment, and his wife would sell everything at the market.

"A worthless good-for-nothing," concluded Ilya Yemelyanovich. "He's dead and good riddance."

And on this occasion, he proposed that we play a game of chess. Ilya Yemelyanovich loved to play chess, was absorbed by the game, and was a wonderful chess player. We played several games, and each time I played too quickly and lost. When I noticed that he had decided to deliberately lose a game to me, I declined to play on, claiming fatigue.

15. Taking leave

It was the spring of 1945. The ninth of May, the Day of Victory, was celebrated with joy at the colony. Everyone was expecting a great amnesty. Only Ilya Yemelyanovich didn't expect it, and I noted that he didn't even yearn for freedom.

"It's quieter here," he said. "It's also a good thing that, in here, they can't arrest you."

He was happy to hear that a petition had been sent regarding my work release.

"That's good. You've got a long sentence. It's a hard one to serve under guard. This way, though, it's like being a civilian employee, only without a family."

But Alma-Ata turned down the petition, and the higher-ups started to treat me differently. I was of no use to them if I required guards.

Soon, in June, I was suddenly informed, "Prepare to move out!" The roundup was short. Before they could lock me up somewhere, I ran to see Ilya Yemelyanovich. He had not expected such an outcome. We had no time for a long conversation. We embraced with tears in our eyes and then parted ways, never to meet again in this lifetime.

March 1970

Ordeal

1. Camp timber-harvesting detached duty

The camp population in the Ili basin increased rapidly in the 1940s. If there was one camp with a thousand hectares of agricultural holdings here before the war, then during the war, a whole Ili Labor Camp Region was organized, extending its reach to hundreds of thousands of hectares.

Here and there, you'd find jokers who risked their freedom by whispering:

"So now there's this Ili Labor Camp Region, next there'll be an Alma-Ata Labor Camp Oblast, followed by...," and the rest was left unsaid.[11]

All residential buildings in these camps were primitive, with adobe walls and roofs covered with reeds with dirt on top. New barracks were required, along with apartments for service personnel and utility outbuildings, but their construction was on hold because of a lack of lumber.

There are marvelous spruce forests in the Alma-Ata oblast. They are located on the northern slops of Zailiysky Alatau, at a vertiginous altitude of about two thousand meters above sea level. High up.

Looking at the woodlands darkening into the distance above, our economic executives would say:

"So near, and yet so far!"

---

[11] The humor here is that eventually, everything will become "Labor Camp."

Before the war, lumber had been brought in by railroad from Siberia. But now, with a war on, the railroads were too busy. Wood had to be obtained locally. With this in mind, the Ministry of Internal Affairs of the Kazakh Republic managed to obtain — via the appropriate authorities — a tract of forest in the upper reaches of the Chilik river, and began to work it.

It arranged, through the Ili Labor Camp Region, a suitable detached duty assignment for between one hundred fifty and two hundred convicts. The first group of loggers was brought there on foot over goat trails. But how would things, clothing, food, and tools be brought to this altitude? They tried to solve this problem for a long time and finally found the answer, obtaining mountain horses from neighboring collective farms and then delivering everything necessary to the destination on horseback.

2. Driving timber down the Chilik river during the 1945 season

During winter, a stock of lumber was laid up using the most primitive means and then brought down from the mountains to places from where it was intended to be floated. Then in spring, during the snowmelt flood, the logs were dumped *en masse* into the river, from where they were supposed to float down into the lower reaches of the same river. There, at an artificial impoundment, the loose lumber was to be combined into timber rafts and then sent to the end customer, the Ili Camp Labor Region, via the large Ili river.

But the problem was that the huge trees, whose butt ends were more than a half-meter wide, were not inclined to float downriver, because with rare exceptions, the entire riverbed was strewn with great heaps of rock that had fallen from the mountain heights as a result of frequent local earthquakes. The gradient in this river is very large (up to 40 meters per kilometer). In unobstructed water, trees would hurtle at high speed. But then some rock blocks the path of the first log, and the log is held fast to the rock. The next log sticks to the first, and so on. This results in a jam, often consisting of several hundred logs. Some of the trees don't go down the main river channel, but enter side streams and hide behind abundant vegetation, such as reeds, buckthorns, and cockspurs.

In order for 1200 cubic meters of lumber (the amount prepared during the winter) to be moved downriver, the camp administration sent two separate labor teams along both banks of the river.

Lumber-driving equipment and organization in the 1945 season were at a primordial stage. The only "equipment" that every convict used was a *stezhok*, the most ancient lever. Every day (there were no days off), guards would take the team to the work place after breakfast, either upstream or downstream, wherever the camp headquarters had relocated. Then the convict foreman would divide the team into crews and assign each crew an "object." Depending on the nature of the "object," people would take their *stezhoks* and go fully clothed into the water and push the stuck logs or, in the case of a jam, climb onto the logs and use those same *stezhoks* to separate lumber from the jam. Logs from broken jams would float downriver until a new jam formed downstream. And the whole process would begin anew.

Each team — on the left and right banks — was situated for a couple of weeks at a site previously selected by the guards, as far from scrub and forest depths as possible to prevent escape.

No artificial cover against inclement weather was provided to the convicts. They were situated directly on the ground under the open sky. Each received a pair of homespun wool blankets, one to spread under, and the other to cover oneself. Several tents for the administration and the guards were set up some distance away. A medical unit and field kitchen were set up not far from them.

Ivan Andrianovich Yarovoy, an engineer, was the head foreman of the teams and a free contractor. I never was able to understand why the Ministry of Internal Affairs involved him in the timber drives, as nothing about these drives — aside from the ubiquitous *stezhoks* — involved any engineering.

Then again, one time he did talk to us for an hour about safety. It was very simple: if you end up in the water while breaking up a jam, use your *stezhok* to join two floating logs and then get on top and ride along, hell and gone.

"And then what?" the convicts would ask, only to be answered immediately by their critically inclined fellows who had already seen many things since the start the drive:

"You know 'then what'! You hang on until the other log breaks your back, or you sink before it happens."

The point was, the teams lost one man for each ten kilometers of lumber drive distance: 18 people died between July and November over a 180 kilometer stretch.

This circumstance did not worry the camp administration; there were no escapes, and convict deaths were appropriately documented.

3. How I ended up on the timber drive

I had been in a prisoner transport from the north to the south as part of a special detail as an agronomist to an agricultural camp. It was the beginning of September. A golden fall.

It was precisely at this time that the commander of the timber drive duty detachment showed up from the Chilik river at the central camp. This commander was not only responsible for the safekeeping of the convicts entrusted to his care, but had willingly assumed responsibility for delivering timber to the end customer according to strictly specified deadlines. He demanded an additional number of convicts to make up for the "natural" attrition of convicts so as to fulfill his assumed socialist obligations to deliver lumber.

"Otherwise," he said, "the lumber will remain stuck in the mountains for the winter."

It was at this moment that the camp commandant was informed that sixty one convicts were arriving at the train station for his disposition. A guard escort had to be sent for them.

And it was these convicts that the commandant decided to send directly from the train to the timber drive, without bringing them by the camp.

"All of them! We'll sort things out over there."

The commandant's word was law.

I was listed as the sixty-first, and happened to be among the "all " that ended up on the timber drive. From the train, we were immediately loaded onto a truck and taken to the work place. It wasn't actually that far away, but it took us three days to get there, because the vehicles broke down and the roads were in bad repair. We were delivered to the next district jail each time, as if per some schedule, and after an exhausting trip over broken roads, everyone happily settled down, as if in a hotel.

Every group was given travel rations. We set off on the road early, rode all day long without eating, and in the evening, we would cook such a porridge that a spoon would stand up straight in it, and then we'd all eat our fill. The squad commander had told us as early as at the railroad station that we'd have no complaints about the food at the timber drive.

"We'll feed you," he said, "up to your... ." And then he used an indecent word that provoked general laughter, particularly among our young female thieves.

All a convict cares about is to have a full stomach. So we rode along with some rising expectations, as if we were going to grandpa's for a visit.

4. My fellow traveling thieves, their description

In this host of young criminals, I was the only political prisoner. The entire cohort normally treated our kind very poorly, scornfully referring to us as "marks."

They thought they were superior to all the rest of the gray mob that was sunk to its eyeballs in sickening labor, provided by God to punish people for their original sin.

They were divided by vocation: among them were pickpockets, housebreakers, fences, counterfeit swindlers, and others. The counterfeit swindlers considered themselves to be professional intellectuals. These were psychologists, intimately familiar with human weaknesses and capable of plucking you clean without inflicting the least discourtesy. They somewhat disdainfully regarded their own kind who engaged in other vocations.

Initially, upon making the acquaintance of this "high-minded" estate, it appears to constitute some kind of Zaporizhian Sich, a primitive communist society unspoiled by anyone or anything, yet. Their strength lies in the peculiar production cooperative of which they were members. And, as well as any organization, theirs has its own gatherings, a club kept secret from bystanders, which they call a "flash-house" (*malina*). And since this organization possesses assets, it has its own common bank, a *khaza*, in which members of this organization directly and systematically place any "haul" from their capers, which is subsequently divided among all the members of the cooperative, regardless of whether they participated in the caper. They are very disciplined among themselves. This coordinated their activities within the collective based on specific yet unwritten standards of mutual behavior.

Their organization is based on mutual trust, and the trust is based on their conviction in the rectitude of their actions and the loyalty of their comrades. A betrayal of trust is considered a serious crime and punished severely. The bonds of the thieves' clan are a powerful element of their mutual support. For an outsider to cause offense to one thief means to cause offense to all thieves, and the offender must be punished without fail.

Despite all this apparent "democracy," all those "noble partisans of the gravy train" are divided into two very unequal parts. On the one hand, there is a small dominating part, consisting of leaders and their immediate retinue. On the other, are the "yellowbirds," as they were contemptuously called by the aristocrats, or *urki*, as they called themselves. The "yellowbirds" comprised the main mass of "coolie labor" that resignedly served the ruling minority.

The boss (they called him "king") is the guru and physical leader of the gang. Typically, this is a man of character who bends the entire crew to his submission, and they trust him implicitly, confident in (from their perspective) his moral worth and in his infallibility. This authority, admittedly, must be earned by committing certain acts, but once it has been earned, it is retained by the "hero" until the end of his days. He is the boss, the leader of his organization. Based on understandings of *what is proper* — of how his wards must live and with what — the boss draws up an action plan for the gang and assigns specific responsibilities to his confederates to achieve that plan. All gang participants acknowledge this person and submissively subordinate themselves to him.

Of the entire "haul" contributed to the *khaza*, the king and his entourage take as much as they need, and the rest is divided equally among the yellowbirds. Such was the "truth" in our "commune" as well.

5. Boris, the *urki* king

We were being transported in a freight car that had been fitted out for hauling "special" cargo, with bars on the windows and a common latrine to serve the needs of both sexes.

I had noticed a young and handsome Mongol of about twenty-five, who had been nourished on fine chow, back in the car. He was surrounded by a small entourage of about five people. He dominated them by his energetic appearance and strong-willed look. Apparently, he was their acknowledged and sovereign king. Young women-thieves kept watch over his needs. They tried to anticipate his wishes and satisfied them immediately.

When we were dumped at the railroad bed, I noticed the king became interested in my person.

"What might have caused this?" I thought to myself. Whatever money I might have had had long been expropriated by the same company, and I was wearing a convict's clothes. I had nothing that normally might attract the attention of thieves looking for somebody to shake down.

When we were loaded into three trucks, he climbed into the same truck I was in, and even sat next to me: not in the seat of honor, up front, by the cab, as was customarily accorded to kings, but in the back, where there is usually a lot of dust and jolting. Along the way he started to ask about my past. I told him that I was a political, had worked as an instructor at a higher educational institute, had spent a year behind bars, and had six more to go.

"Yes," he said amiably between his teeth. "It'll be hard for you. A difficult ordeal. You are not prepared for this."

Then he started to tell me about himself. It turned out his father was also an instructor at some educational institution somewhere in Siberia, maybe Krasnoyarsk, or maybe Irkutsk — a lecturer in chemistry. When we were pulling up to the next "hotel," he finished by saying:

"I want to talk with you some more."

Once, while our regular thick porridge was being cooked in the prison yard for us hungry "tourists," Boris (that's what they called the king) again came up to me. He sat down next to me and confessed his sins to me for a long time.

At the age of twelve, captivated by a romantic yearning for a change of scenery, he ran away from home, fell in with thieves, and had been living like that for thirteen years, sometimes at large, sometimes in jail. He admitted that by the age of twenty-five, his former romanticism had melted away, and now he wanted to live peacefully, start a family, and reconcile with his parents.

In short, Boris had decided to "wind it up," as camp convicts say. Apparently, this process of moral rebirth had progressed far with him, and he had selected me to be a deserving intermediary in the rapprochement with his parents. He finished his confession by saying:

"I will not let you come to harm in the camp. Remember that."

Apparently, Boris had thought through the question of how to get rid of his closest henchmen there, in the camp. I saw him talking for a long time with the troop commander.

After we arrived at the left-bank team headquarters on the left bank and the newcomers had been sorted, it turned out that Boris, I, and another 28 predominantly female yellowbirds had been selected for the right bank. The entire more "experienced" part, capable of escape, remained on the left bank with the troop commander, in an improvised zone enclosed with barbed wire. There was no such zone on the right bank. The zone there was conventional, and its boundaries consisted of individual boulders, growing trees, bushes, and the river bank.

"Any convict passing beyond such a marker without the permission of the guards, will be considered as attempting to escape. The guards will open fire on offenders without warning!" announced senior sergeant Zenin, the all-powerful assistant troop commander on the right bank, as his final order to us.

By the way, all of this "strictness" applied only to nighttime; during daylight, after work, you could go wherever you wanted and fetch anything at all.

Having earmarked the right-bank convict group, the troop commander allowed us to move to the right-bank camp by ourselves over a bridge that was located about a kilometer downstream of where we were.

Boris, who had been gladdened by the fact that we would now be together, walked next to me and told me of how the internal life of thieves was arranged. It was all as I have set forth above.

Suddenly, the troop commander caught up with us on his horse. It turned out that Boris's friends had rebelled over his having been separated from them and had demanded his return, and that if he were not returned, they wouldn't turn up for work.

It was apparent that, for the first time in his life, Boris lost his bearings. You could see that he really didn't want to go back, but he knew the thieves' law. Looking at me intently, as if expecting advice, he stretched out his arm.

"Well! What can you do?" he said, and then turned and went back.

That was our last meeting.

After both teams had run the logs along the main river channel, some were still left in some of its parts, having been jammed into the thick vegetation in the numerous channels of the Chilik. Although thieves, once in a camp, go by the saying "don't work but don't let them see you not working", Boris, stuck on the left bank, decided to work. He organized his entourage into a group of five people and, giving his word of honor that his people wouldn't escape anywhere, followed the teams for six weeks, cleaning stuck logs out of channels.

By the middle of October, his group had managed to run their logs to a 20-meter-high waterfall. There was a small jam at the waterfall itself. It had to be taken apart so as to enable the logs to drop about sixty feet down all at once. It was coming up to the time for the midday meal, so they decided to take a smoke break so that later, after busting up the jam, they could go immediately to where lunch was being delivered. Everyone lay down on the bank. Boris sat by himself, also smoking, hunkered on a thick log hanging by a thread at the edge of the precipice.

Suddenly, a log showed up out of nowhere and bumped the log that the group leader was sitting on. The whole jam broke up; logs started falling down from a 20-meter height, and Boris fell with them. Looking into the seething stream, his comrades only saw that Boris' arms were flapping about like ropes. He could not fight the elements, and soon disappeared under the water.

He was dressed in cotton pants, wadding, and felt boots, and wore a tight belt around himself. On the third day, his body was recovered about twelve kilometers from the place where he died. He had been completely undressed by the water and his arms were broken. None of the *urki* went to work during his funeral. The next day, I happened to see his grave, which for some reason was located on our right bank. It was all covered in flowers.

He never managed to tell me the names of his parents. Of course, nobody informed them of this tragic incident. They do not know how their prodigal son, who at the end of his life dreamt of returning to the lap of his parents, had died ignominiously.

6. First acquaintance in a new place

Somewhat discouraged that I had been abandoned by my former protector, I continued on my way alone. Broken up into small groups, my companions moved in the same direction, but at different speeds: you could see how the vanguard was already approaching the tents that could be seen in the distance, while others had only just crossed the bridge. It had been a long time since I had been allowed to walk freely, at my own pace, with no guard, so I was enjoying this journey. True, we had been warned in advance that there was a *secret post* somewhere downstream, which vigilantly kept track of convict movements. But that post and its secrets were irrelevant to us. There were such posts at the boundaries of our Motherland, as well. Who perceives them? Moreover, where would we run, and to whom? To the left and right of the river were topless mountain crests, upstream there were those same crests capped with white glaciers. Downstream was the post.

Approaching the camp site, I noticed a person sitting under a torn piece of canvas with one corner tied to a scraggly hawthorn bush and two other corners tied to different spots on a huge boulder. He looked at me inquisitively. He apparently knew that a new transport of prisoners had arrived. And a new transport always brought new acquaintances, and news. I made my way toward him.

"Sit down and rest," he said politely, indicating a log lying near his tent and flashing a dozen gold teeth.

He was a man of 40 to 50 years of age, of strong physique, with an elongated, well-shaved, sunburned, and well-fed face.

Having asked me about who I had been in the past, the article I had been sentenced under, and how long my sentence was, he informed me:

"Things look bad. The work's not hard, but it's very dangerous. It's a mountain river, serpentine, and the water's cold. It's snowy. And just last week we lost someone," he concluded and looked at me. Then he told me something of himself. In his time, he also nearly ended up in jail for the article I was in for, but managed to wriggle free. And now, he even felt regret, as it was an honorable article to be convicted under. Now, he was serving a sentence under some other article but didn't say what it was. He was a Muscovite, himself, and had been working in the camp as a barber and, in addition, in his free time, ran pack horses loaded with bread to and from a nearby collective farm.

"In short," he said, "as long as I'm considered a nutcase, they don't make me go into the water."

It was right before the midday meal, and all the convicts were working somewhere offsite. Besides the first nutcase, I noticed in the distance, in the shade of a huge boulder, two fine fellows occasionally striking something with hammers. It turned out they were shoemakers. As that same barber explained to me, they were supposed to return home soon under the most recent amnesty. A woman cook tinkered about at a fire closer to the guards' tents. She had an outdoor kitchen, and the canvas shelter was for the products, in case of rain. The only nurse, herself a convict, worked in a small tent not far from the large guard tents. It was said that final diagnosis and release from work were not hers to make, but assistant troop commander sergeant Zenin's, who ruled this part of the world.

Among all these structures, homespun wool blankets lay sprawled over a relatively large area. These were the beds of the convicts. Here, the convicts spent the night under the open sky, protected by nothing but hole-ridden flimsy blankets.

Right before lunch, from the left-bank headquarters to the tents went a man in military uniform with red epaulets showing one broad stripe. He had an important look, wore whiskers, and was about 55 years old; according to the senior warder on the right bank, this was our direct chief, who kept track of our behavior and fostered us with socially beneficial labor. When the man came closer, I even experienced a fright: as alike as two peas, he resembled the Kremlin Master who everyone worshiped in those days.

"What do you think, there's a resemblance, no?" asked me the barber immediately.

It turned out that my new acquaintance was not just a barber. He was an artist. He was able, over some time, to take this comely Ukrainian, with his black hair and streaks of gray, and create such a hideous thing using only his instruments.

"If you like," said this artist, carefully examining me, "I could make a Voroshilov[12] out of you in a month. How about it?"

The warder, apparently, was pleased with his likeness. He would act important in front of the convicts, give speeches like that other, tongue-tied but long with a heavy accent, albeit in the Ukrainian style. He immediately assembled all the "fresh meat," formed them in one rank, and counted them. Everyone was present.

Then and there, we were issued the same bedding, a pair of gray blankets made of coarse goat hair, and then we were fed. We were fed pretty well even later, receiving a kilo of bread each, a bowl of borsch with meat as a first course, and American pork spam as a second course. Apparently, the camp command had specified such a diet

---

[12] Kliment Yefremovich Voroshilov (1881-1969) held the rank of Marshal and was People's Commissar for Defense. One of Stalin's few trusted henchmen, Voroshilov personally signed nearly 200 documented execution lists.

from the upper-level command, so as to keep the convicts from attempting to escape.

The senior warder — we all called him Vusa — did not play the key administrative role on the right bank. That role belonged to assistant troop commander, sergeant Zenin. He represented the local legislative branch. All plans for the upcoming day — how many were to go to what places with which guards, and so on — were drawn up in his tent, from which he emerged only rarely. The warder, despite his frightful appearance, represented the local executive branch. He was, so to speak, our relief commander.

Zenin was an extremely unbalanced individual. It was as if there were two Zenins. Sometimes he would forget about his local role and become benign, jocular, talkative, and mawkishly lenient with convicts, especially the women. But then he'd remember who he was and where he was, and then he would become vociferous and intolerably loud, promising to lock certain convicts up in the cooler as soon as they return to the camp center. At times like this he became the most typical of petty tyrants. For now, he was only a sergeant, but if his epaulets were to take on some shiny stars[13], what might happen then?

7. We work on the timber drive

At sunset, the team of timber drivers would return from working at a location to night quarters. The team comprised Russians and Kazakhs collected for the drive from the closest district jails, recently convicted primarily of theft of socialist property. These were collective farmers. This was

---

[13]   Stars are used on Soviet military rank insignia to denote officers.

not that aristocracy of professional thieves with whom I arrived here.

Tired, some of them soaked to their waists, they hauled back armfuls of the dry brushwood that lay scattered on the river bank and, as soon as they returned to camp, they started fires and began to dry out.

I peered at their harsh faces and immediately experienced a feeling of deep respect for them.

"And so," thought I, "there was a time when the intelligentsia would go among the people, and not understanding them, would try to beckon them to rivers of milk and banks of honey. But here, what fortune! I'm right next to that same crowd, on common ground."

Happening to be next to me, a local loner-thief confirmed, just before we all went to sleep, the unpleasant news that I had received earlier.

"I've served stretches before," he said, "but I've never yet stumbled into such a scrape. Right now, they're still laughing and talking all around us. But if you listen in the morning, there's absolute silence, because people keep wondering whether they'll be coming back in the evening and who this awful river will claim next."

Then he thought for a while and confided, in a whisper:

"It's worth trying to escape. A new sentence is better than dying here," and then he turned over and immediately fell asleep.

Soon, the remaining convicts fell silent as well, as fatigue and fresh air did their work. Only quiet voices could be heard not far away, of the female thieves who had arrived with me. Try as they might, they could not fall asleep. They didn't yet understand the kind of "flash-house" that awaited them here.

Along the edges of this battlefield sown with bodies there burned the occasional small fires. These were for the duty military guards who were going to work after having slept during the day. Now, during the night, they were responsible for the safekeeping of 90 convicts.

The next day, I was placed in a group consisting of four people and began to "bust my gut" using the same *stezhok*, that all of the coolie labor had been issued. We were given an "object" to work on in the morning, after which we would try to "crack" the latest nut without having anyone hurry us along. Soon I became convinced that quite a bit of time could be spent on a single task, and that through profound reflection, it could be completed over a very short time with a minimum expenditure of physical labor. For example, when breaking apart a jam, you can push it by removing one tree at a time from it, and so on, to the last one, or you can feel about for the point where the whole mass of logs is balanced and start precisely with that point, and then the whole jam might fall apart at once into its individual parts and they'll drift away downstream. But this stepwise transition from one state (a jam) to another (of logs drifting off individually) hides within itself a terrible danger for people. Not one timber driver who fell into the water with a loosened jam emerged from the river alive, because logs, traveling at different speeds depending on their size and weight, would crash against each other with terrible force, and if there was a human between them when that happened, the result would be the loss of the arm being used to hang on to a log, or a broken back. Everything depended on what side of the log the person was located. After receiving an injury, he can no longer control his body and sinks to the bottom.

Not all timber drivers break up jams. There is "easier" work as well. Reaches form in places where the riverbed widens, and here the water flows slowly and it's a little more than knee-deep. It's in such reaches that the heavy logs don't want to float further. They either crawl along the river bottom or stop completely after encountering some obstacle.

Women and overweary men were sent to the reaches, because this was the easiest and least dangerous work. Workers in clothing and shoes spent their entire day pushing logs with long sticks. But the water was so cold that the feet turned numb, and they must be taken out of the water one at a time and held in the warm air until they recover. At least it was that way in September and the first half of October. Later in the year, when during the night the logs would become covered in hoarfrost and water would freeze at their edges, legs would feel warmer in the water than in the air.

You are still alive. You've not been seized by a whirlpool. But what kind of life is this? By nightfall, the cold water has bloated your legs to the point where you can barely take off your footwear. At night, the rafters warm their outer extremities at the fires. It feels better. But then it starts to rain. The convicts have nowhere to get out of the rain. They only each have a pair of blankets with so many holes in them, they resemble nets. They cover themselves with them and huddle together, like herring in a barrel, and lie down right on the bare ground. The rain goes on for days and all this time the convicts remain on the ground, wet, hungry, and angry.

8. I manage my everyday life

On the very first night, on the timber drive, I felt all of the inconveniences of the night's stop. So, upon returning from work, I began to build myself a shelter. I collected deadwood that was scattered near the water and used it to erect a frame. Then I took a scythe from the stableman and cut reeds of various grass, and covered the entire structure with this green mass. Inside the hut, I laid down an ample bed made of dried grass. In the morning, I'd arise with fully recovered strength. Between the relatively good food, the fresh air, and physical labor, I gained strength and became healthier.

I thought it interesting that nobody else among the convicts followed my example. Upon returning to base, they would immediately topple down to sleep, often in still-damp clothes.

Every ten or fifteen days, we would relocate to a new place, and every time, that first day, I would build myself a shelter using many of the parts from my previous shelters. When it rained, the convicts lay down in a compact ring around my shelter, as though it helped them. But I alone was inside the hut, dry and warm. As long as it rained, many got ready to build themselves shelters. But as soon as the rain went away, so did their good intentions.

After several rainy days, an artist who has already been introduced — the barber — started to ask entrance to my residence. We expanded my structure somewhat and began to live in it together.

To my misfortune, whenever it was the turn of our warder — Vusa — to perform camp duty, he would come up to my hut, position himself near my head, roll a "goat's leg" stogie with shag tobacco, and then start endless conversations about this and that.

From my file, he had learned that I was agronomist. Before joining the army, he had worked as a gardener on a collective farm. And it was this one circumstance that drew him to me like a magnet.

"Life's funny that way," he told me. "Out in the world, you would have been my boss, but here — " he didn't finish the sentence and changed the subject to raising seedlings in hothouses, to plant diseases and how to deal with them, and so on and so forth.

I also made the mistake at the very start of our "friendship" of telling him, as a Ukrainian, something of the history of the Zaporizhian Sich. This only heightened his interest in me and it seemed almost as if he eagerly looked forward to his duty so as to again come by my hut and immerse himself in the old times of Zaporizhian freedom.

"No," I would finally tell him, "you can sleep tomorrow during the day, but I've got to go work." And I came to a halt on the recently elected Hetman Taras Tryasil, trailed off, and tried to fall asleep as quickly as I could. He also trailed off. But later, when I was almost asleep, he started on about something of his own, sounding off on the corruption of the Poles and the unfaithfulness of the Crimean khans.

Occasionally, I would also meet with our foreman, Ivan Andrianovich. He alternated his lodgings in the guard tents, on the left and the right banks. Each time he told me, as if apologizing, that he could not find a way to set me up in some safe place, expressed regret that I had no other specialty apart from timber driver, and that if this had been the camp center, he would be able to do something for me. Then he praised himself on how he had been able to set Dubrovskiy up there as the bath supervisor, and then as the barber, and so on.

I thanked Ivan Andrianovich for his interest in me, but replied that I was satisfied with my work and would not leave for some place warm. He merely spread wide his arms.

The romance of timber driving had captured me nonetheless. Our team learned to quickly dismantle the most intricate obstructions and to get off of them in time, before these disordered bunches of logs suddenly toppled into the water. This was very dangerous. No less dangerous was the icy water, which gradually degraded the health of the timber drivers. I understood all of this very well and decided to take steps so as to leave this cursed Chilik behind in the near future. I had to write, to make noise, to ask. But to my horror, there wasn't a scrap of paper anywhere in the camp.

One evening, we were returning from work as a team. On the left side of the path, about 30 meters from it, I noticed something in the grass, flapping in the wind.

"Paper!" I thought to myself, and asked the guard for permission to go get it. It turned out to be a scrap of thick wallpaper, which had been used by someone for a slogan banner. The letters had been washed away by rain, and the paper itself had darkened. But I was happy to have even this scrap. At the base, I wrote a letter to my wife and asked her to immediately send a request to the relevant authorities that I be transferred to an agricultural camp to work in my specialty. When the wife of one of the Kazakhs arrived for a conjugal visit, I asked her to drop my letter in the nearest post box. I had no idea if she understood my request or if she would comply. Still, now there was something to wait for.

9. The death of the young Kazakh woman Fatima

Driving timber along a mountain river that had not previously been cleared of various obstructions is like life on a military front. Mortal danger threatens the timber driver even at places where it is least expected. Generally speaking, timber driving is a man's work, and I was surprised when I saw women engaged in it.

A beautiful young Kazakh woman named Fatima, from a neighboring jail, had ended up on the timber drive. As she explained, her husband was helping take Berlin and would soon return home. She lived with her husband's mother and two young children, and worked on the collective farm. The head of the collective farm — a large, overweight lecher whose eyes had become swollen from excess fat — had begun to hit on her and she had rejected him. As a result, he harbored ill feelings for her and ordered his snitches to catch Fatima committing some kind of "crime." When she returned from a field where she had been reaping wheat with other women, they searched her and found a little more than a kilo of grain in her pockets, which she had taken while working, so as to feed her mother-in-law and children. Since none of the collective farm workers had received much of anything at all over many years for their days of labor, they all "stole" a little of everything at work. If they didn't, they would have died of hunger long ago. But the order was given: theft of socialist property was formalized with a proper certificate. Judgment was then passed on Fatima, who, condemned, was sent to the timber drive.

Now she worked hard with a *stezhok,* together with the others, and was being re-educated through socially beneficial labor. She did not take obstructions apart, but she spent entire days in the water, burrowing around the largest logs that had become hung up on something, so that they might float further downstream on their own.

Here's Ush-Aral, a natural landmark. Here, the ridges have diverged far from each other and the river spreads out very wide. The river's depth is just below the knee. Not enough. Logs that have floated down to here are incapable of continuing on their way by themselves. They need to be nudged. So here's Fatima, working with her women's section. Over the course of the day, they have become burned out from the endless pushing. This one thick log in particular had no desire to submit to the women. One point of it sat on some bottom feature. When Fatima got downstream of the log and did something with her *stezhok,* the log suddenly tore free, sweeping Fatima underneath and rolling over her. Her bones remained unbroken; she experienced only deep scratches and bruising. In the evening, she went to see the nurse. The nurse excused her from work for one day. In the morning, after reveille, Fatima remained lying in her bed. Zenin, the duty assistant timber drive commander that morning, loudly burst into angry words — you could hear him throughout the camp

— regarding Fatima's absence, then he went to her "bed," ripped the blanket from her, and ordered her to immediately take her place in the team's pre-work formation. Frightened of the furious cur, she jumped up in what she was wearing, threw on a cotton coat, and fell in.

That same Zenin ordered Fatima's section to cross to the left bank, using the ford located immediately next to the encampment. The fording was done on horseback. An elderly Kazakh, astride a horse, would cross the river first, leading other horses that ferried people across the river with a rope. Just as Fatima got to the center of the river on horseback, she fell head-down into the water with almost no reaction, and went to the bottom. At first, you could see the flaps of her coat and her long hair, which were spread out by the water.

And then Fatima was no more.

Zenin, who had observed all of this, suddenly drew his pistol and fired twice into the air. "Emergency!" he says. "Escape!" The only thing is, he wasn't shooting where he should have. Instead of the sky, he should have put a bullet through his temple. It would have been more honest.

What happened next, we don't know. The children were left motherless. Apparently, her husband returned from the front, but Fatima was gone. She was the seventeenth victim of the high-handedness and violence that reigned here. She was written off as easily as the preceding sixteen people, and Zenin even earned another stripe. There have been no escapes from the camp. Everything was in order.

10. I go under

As my luck had it, Vusa wasn't on duty the previous night, so I got a good night's sleep. That morning, we were assigned a treacherous jam. Its treachery lay in the fact that it occurred about 50 meters upstream of a huge waterfall. This meant that if you fell into the water with the suddenly released obstruction, you had only about 50 meters in which to maneuver and save yourself. If that short span was not used to full advantage, death was certain.

There was a small granite island remnant to the right of the river's shallows. The mass of water approaching the shallows fell downward with a great noise, while the other part of the water bore down on the remnant and, scouring its left and right sides, also crashed down, together with the logs. The island could become a barrier to logs that floated against it, and a jam could form near it.

As if foreboding disaster, I studied the entire possible situation in advance. Then our section as a whole inspected the jam and made sure that it was in alignment, forming a kind of lever with arms of equal length that were subjected to the force of rapidly flowing water, and that it was held in equilibrium, with the right-hand arm resting slightly on the shore. Just the left-hand arm needed to be lengthened to disrupt this equilibrium. The water's force would turn the jam about its axis, so it could — having lost its equilibrium — crash into the water with all its mass. With this goal in mind, we began to roll free logs from the right-hand arm to the left. After this, the jam began to shake and shiver. Some additional logs needed to be added to the left-hand side, and the water would do its work.

We took a smoke break before the decisive attack. Before the final assault, I took off my warm clothing (it was cold) and was dressed in only my underwear.

As we were pushing the last log onto the left-hand side, I got carried away and forgot about the danger. As we expected, the water operated quickly. It turned the jam by 60 degrees and it began to fall apart into separate logs. My comrades, who were closer to the shore, managed to make it to land, while I fell into the water.

I had several times seen how, in such circumstances, people had ended up in the water and how, after making what appeared to onlookers to be some haphazard motions and receiving injuries from the logs, they quickly sank to the bottom. I knew that all of my seventeen predecessors had not returned from the water, and that I was the eighteenth victim.

At that moment, I forgot about everything in the world. It was as if I had neither wife, nor children, nor parents, nor did the camp exist, either. Only I and my frightful and implacable environment were left in the whole world. I had only a few minutes to think and quickly make a decision. I decided that I'd need to move directly to the island along with suitable logs. But some logs being carried by the water currents were moving directly to the lethal precipice, others were moving to the island, while a third group bypassed the island on the right and fell into the cascade beyond. I maneuvered, diving under logs, appearing at the surface of those logs that were headed for the island. I understood that the island, too, was a danger to life. So here's a log that I've grabbed hold of, that's floating relatively slowly right to the island. But having gotten within a dozen meters of the island, the log suddenly picks up considerable speed and crashes with all its weight against the logs that have already gotten stuck on the island. Afterward, other logs stick with the same speed and the same roar, and so on. They don't wait to see if you've gotten out of the water or are still on the log, and they'll rattle your spine in such a way as to cleave body and soul (if the previous log hasn't already broken your arms).

To avoid all of this rough going, I decided to use the inertia of the water. As I approached the shore of the island at high speed on the log, I threw my arms up and slid along the surface of the logs that were there. Immediately behind me, I heard the screeching of logs floating up to the island. But I was beyond their reach.

I had conquered the elements! I was seized by a feeling of joy. I, like Robinson Crusoe, was now the only one on the island. I gained my feet, looked around, remembered my wife and children, and wept sweet tears. They were tears of victory.

While I was in the water, I heard some shooting from the shore, and cries from the same shore. But I was too distracted to pay attention. How could they help me, anyway?

But I was on the island, and it was dangerous to attempt to get to the shore by myself. From the island, I saw how Ivan Adrianovich rushed about on shore, organizing something. When the last logs of our jam passed me, and the water cleared, a young Kazakh rode up to the bank with a lasso. Advancing as far as he could into the water, he sat on his horse and tried to throw me the end of the lasso. Unfortunately, the lasso could not reach me. If he tried to come closer to the island, the water would cause the horse he was on to lose its footing. Nevertheless, after several attempts, I held the end of the lasso in my hand. I tied it around my waist, threw myself into the icy water, and ended up on the bank without injury and in one piece.

No, I had no wish to become the eighteenth victim. Aleksandr Strukov, a machinist convicted during the Alma-Ata Railroad Wreckers' Trial, would become the eighteenth and last victim somewhat later.

11. I pass the test to become a cobbler

Ivan Andrianovich met me on the shore.

"Well, I thought you were a goner!" he said, sympathetically. "You're a fine lad, a fine lad! You've passed the test with an 'A'!

From what he was saying, I understood that he was claiming credit for himself for saving me, which I was able to do thanks to his safety lectures.

"It was a fine test," I replied. "Of the eighteen that took it, only I passed it."

But Ivan Andrianovich didn't understand my dig.

As it turned out, in saving myself from certain death, I *had* put Ivan Andrianovich's safety techniques to the test. As he had suggested, I had tried to join two adjacent floating logs with my *stezhok* and tried to float on them, but the logs were of different size, and one of them broke free and floated away. Selecting logs by weight while you're in the water was completely impossible. I threw away my *stezhok* and began to act using my own safety technique.

After taking a bath in that terrible Chilik baptismal font, I was chilled. The head foreman invited me into his tent and gave me a glass of vodka. Coming somewhat to my senses, I told him:

"So, Ivan Andrianovich, before this dunking, I was one person; now I am another. That one died, he drowned. Everything that my predecessors experienced I endured on my own hide. I have a family of no small size, and I must think of them. I don't want to go back into the water. Let me be a cobbler."

"But do you know how to do the work?" he asked me, with a gentle smile. "Why didn't you tell me about that before? We have an acute need for cobblers."

"I kept it secret. I didn't want my comrades to reproach me, saying, hey, he's become scared of the water. Now, after what happened, nobody will say anything."

I was ordered to draw a cobbler's tool from the camp steward and start work immediately, since after the previous cobblers had been released under an amnesty, quite a lot of ragged footwear had accumulated in the camp.

That evening, sergeant Zenin's hysterical voice could be heard inside the commander's tent where the following day's plan was being worked out. He had apparently learned from Ivan Andrianovich that I was now engaged in a new role.

"What kind of cobbler is he, that pointy-head? He's been frightened by the water. What a highbrow!" he yelled.

And so before long, a Kazakh guard comes up to my hut carrying almost new army boots with the sole torn away at the toe, and a piece of flat rubber that had been cut from an automobile tire and flattened under a hot press.

"Here," he said, giving me a work order. "These boots need to be taken in, made smaller, and have the soles replaced with these," he showed me the rubber.

My hut mate was on a trip, visiting the collective farm. I was alone and could not fall asleep for some time. All the while, I was thinking: How do I attach the flattened rubber to the boots so that it holds fast? Incidentally, the rifleman, the owner of the boots, was a hunter, and spent a lot of time among the mountain rocks, so he needed particularly rugged boots.

Naturally, I understood that this first commission was a test for me.

"If he fails, he goes right back to the water!" hissed Zenin, as was later told to me.

After I had thought through the entire process of taking in the army boots down to the last detail, I fell asleep.

The next morning, I was not bothered by the first bell for reveille. I ate breakfast only after the entire team had already left for work. I'm no longer some kind of common rabble. I am a cobbler! See what we can do, Zenin!

After breakfast, I drew a couple of bags of cobbler's stock from the steward and set myself up under a lone tree like a new production unit.

Just between us, I was far from a beginner in the shoe business. Back during the first world war, and later, during the years of the revolution, when our industry had been paralyzed and the shops were empty, my granddad and I spent summers preparing hides for uppers and soles, and winters cobbling shoes for the entire family. The footwear was simple but rugged, and was sewn using one last for both feet. The basics of the cobbler's trade were nothing new to me. Of course, that had been a quarter century ago, but knowledge isn't something you wear on your back.

I tore apart the soldier's boots, soaked the uppers and stretched them on the proper last, and I didn't nail the uppers slipshod to the insole, the way Stakhanovite cobblers did later, but used my granddad's method and sewed them tight with cobbler's thread. At the same time, I sewed a rand to the insole, and then I cut a pair of soles from the rubber square and used the same thread to sew them to the rand, hiding the thread in a concealed seam I had cut in the sole. The heels, as was proper, I attached tightly using nails. The only task left was to make them look good. The main thing was to cut the edges of the soles evenly. But the tire rubber submitted poorly to the knife, and the rasp didn't work well, either. Suddenly, an idea occurred to me, and if it was successful, it would be quite a discovery! I heated a couple of iron scraps in the fire until they were crimson, and then ran them along the edges of the sole after first covering the uppers with a wet rag. The edge of the sole became wonderfully even, and the rubber adhered to the rand so well, than you couldn't tell where the rubber ended and the leather started.

That evening, when the escort guards returned from work, I took the finished boots to the guards' tent. My customer was so impressed with the quality of the work, that he immediately took a small key from his belt, opened his footlocker, and presented me with a kilogram tin of American spam. This was my first income from my cobbler's specialty. Meanwhile, the boots were passed around among the guards. Everyone admired my work.

And so I had passed my cobbler's test and saved myself from having to work on the timber drive. Zenin had nothing he could trump me with.

12. I am a tinsmith. Business.

Winter gradually arrived. Overnight, logs would become covered with thick hoarfrost. Along their edges, icicles would form where they met the water. Water standing in little pools would become covered with thin layers of ice.

People were terribly cold, especially at night under the open sky. Management went off somewhere, trying to do something.

It was said that the mountains came to an end around a dozen kilometers distant. After that, the terrain was flat.

We made one more move. I was not able to build my hut in time and, like everyone else, lay down with my new friend, dear Yuriy Ivanovich Udod, on the ground under the open sky. Cooperation is a blessing. Instead of one, we spread a pair of blankets under ourselves and covered ourselves with two more. By morning, we felt some weight on top of us. Snow had fallen during the night and covered us. Here, soon after dawn, someone brought news: felt boots had just been brought in and they were being issued over there, under that cliff. A line formed. Many stood in the snow barefoot. That was okay. They would soon be warm; there were felt boots to be had.

By lunch, all of us, now the combined two teams, moved to the flatland and settled into a collective farm's dairy barns (the livestock was still summering somewhere). There were no windows or doors anywhere, but things were already looking up because there was a roof over our heads.

I set myself up with my cobbler's shop in a calf shack with one window. What privilege! Such happiness was not available to all. I used the bags that held my cobbler's stock to make something like curtains for the window and door. In one corner, closer to the window, I used hand-formed brick to make something like a fireplace and ran the flue right out the window. Never before or later did I feel so well-furnished as in that memorable shack.

The food they gave us became significantly worse. But still, each of us received one hundred grams of American spam as a second course. The spam resulted in the growth of a mountain of empty cans next to the kitchen. In the center of the farm there was a huge tractor-drawn plow, from before the war, with a rear housing that had been screwed off and a frame that partially jutted from the back.

"There's that marvelous tin from the cans, this piece of the plow can be a straightening tool, plus a little knowledge..." I thought to myself. "Might there be some business to be done?"

I got a pair of ordinary scissors from the farm director's wife and set to work. The tin was soft and easily worked. The first thing I did was make a soup ladle and give it to the farm director's wife as a gift. I made a few more and gave them as gifts to her friends, who visited her from the neighboring village.

Soon, word about me had spread throughout the vicinity. I was overwhelmed with customers. As it turned out, they considered a soup ladle to be an object of luxury. Above all, they had no utensils in which to cook food, as they had all worn through during the war years. The ladles had their effect. They were the start of my business. I widely announced that my enterprise repaired pots, but only if they had small holes. (Hey, there wasn't enough material to repair large holes!)

So as not to undermine my credibility, I didn't make known the extreme simplicity of my process. I would clinch the holes with tin rivets that I had prepared in advance, so the entire repair would take a minute or two of work time. I did not repair the utensils in front of the customer, but would carefully inspect it, place it to the side, and announce:

- "*Dzharaid! Tan ertyn.*" (Which meant in Kazakh, "Okay, I'll do it. It'll be ready tomorrow morning.")

I didn't count the number of pots that passed through my hands. It was a deluge. I had no set rates for the work. Whatever you care to give, well, that's okay. I was paid in kind with milk, corn meal, squash, and my appearance at that time was such that it's a shame I didn't have a camera.

I repaired all of the small holes in the pots. Then, in response to special customer requests (if the customer's pleas were reasonable, from my point of view; for example, if there wasn't a single pot in the house with only a small hole), I'd repair large holes and place new bottoms in pails.

Naturally, I completed all of my shoe-repair work quickly and scrupulously. River drivers without footwear are not river drivers. Eventually, I acquired such power in the camp that even Zenin shut up, and I never heard another word from him in my direction.

13. I teach mathematics as a *mugalim*

As the reader already knows, a director lived on the farm with his family. He was a Kazakh who had recently returned from Germany after the end of the war. My acquaintance with him began on a business basis.

There wasn't a single sound cow-milking pail on his farm. True, they had all been repaired previously by some local sage. The repair technique could not have been simpler. A wooden circle the size of the pail's diameter was cut, and then it was inserted where previously there had been a tin bottom. Nails were used to prevent the circle from moving around, but after such a repair, the pail could only be used for granular substances. To hold liquid, all of the cracks were stuffed with wool, but this didn't help much. In the center of the area where cows were milked, there was an ordinary can into which the milk was poured. The milkmaid would milk at a rapid pace into a leaky pail, and then run over to the can and pour out what remained of the milk. A large amount of milk was lost, and naturally, there was a mess. The farm director implored me to repair several pails for the farm. And I did.

Afterward, problems arose in his family. His only son Yermek, whom he adored, had failed mathematics in the fifth grade of the Kazakh middle school and had been left back to repeat the grade. The father asked me if I could help his son.

Yermek spoke no Russian at all. My ability to speak Kazakh was scant, to put it mildly. From the boy's notebooks of the previous year, I determined that he knew the basic four operations well and correctly solved problems with decimal division, but couldn't cope with common fractions. He had not understood them from the beginning. He did not understand what a numerator was, or a denominator.

Having devised a wordless method for teaching simple fractions, I began to work with Yermek in the evenings in his apartment.

We began with the most simple: we tore an ordinary notebook into its components, counted the number of sheets, and wrote down that number. These were the integers. Then I took one sheet and tore it in half. I counted the halves, and wrote their quantity in the denominator and one whole sheet in the numerator. He then understood what was meant by one half. Then we tore that same page again into quarters, counted them, and wrote their quantity in the denominator. He quickly satisfied himself as to why a fraction with identical numbers in the numerator and denominator was equal to one. Then he cut up a sheet himself and worked with the pieces.

In short, Yermek understood where fractions come from and how to operate with them. Operations with compound fractions seemed to him a total discovery.

Each time Yermek and I would sit down at the round table and start to work, his mother would be cooking dinner. When she set the table, the lessons ended. At the table, Yermek would attend to me. He would select the tastiest morsels from the dishes and serve them to me.

"*Mugalim, oh mugalim!*" he said, in his language. "Teacher."

His father spoke Russian relatively well. He had recently returned from Germany and what he had seen still impressed him. From Germany, he, as a victor, had brought a small bag of various German buttons. They were all of different size and color. Usually after dinner, he would empty the little bag onto the table and the family would begin to examine these trophies. He had also brought one rope he had cut from a German horse collar. How it had impressed the conqueror, I did not understand. Apparently, it was the thickness of the leather.

Yermek and I finished the program within a month. He passed the exam and went on to attend school in the same grade as his friends. However, Yermek continued to invite me to dinner every day, as before. He was as attentive to me at the table as before. It was a shame that language separated us, because our spirits were very close.

14. Stockpiling timber and moving back to the camp center

The camp command failed to complete the timber drive assignment within the stated deadline. The mouth of the river was another fifty kilometers or so away, and winter was setting in. There was a danger of the logs freezing into the river, from where no expedition would be able to haul them out. And then in spring, during the snowmelt flood, they would indeed float themselves downstream and might turn up somewhere in Lake Balkhash. Then all the labor of one season of work by the forest camp detachment would be lost. For this reason, the commanders decided, headlong, to drive the logs into a special impoundment and begin stockpiling them on the shore. The most physically healthy individuals were assigned to stockpiling, while the rest drove the logs to the impoundment.

My former shelter tenant, our illustrious perriquier Leonid Fedorovich Dubrovskiy, heard from someone that our detachment headquarters, in light of the critical situation, had decided to force everyone into the water, including himself, the barber, who feared the timber drive with mortal dread.

This announcement didn't scare me, although it affected me as well. The need for such a decisive step as the stockpiling of timber was evident, while physically I felt as though I even wanted to exert myself somewhat.

For Dubrovskiy, who believed that "this cup" had passed him by, such news was terrible. He didn't sleep all night. By morning, he had come up with a plan that he shared with me when he woke me at dawn.

"Listen, dear Aleksandr Konstantinovich. Just once, at my request, become a snitch, although I know how unfavorably you regard this activity. You're on friendly terms with Vusa, and whether I live or die depends on him. This very morning, drop a whisper in his direction that so and so, Dubrovskiy knows that they want to send him to work on the team, that he didn't sleep all night, and finally decided to take an ax to you if you even hint about working on the team.

Leonid Fedorovich believed this "game" to be the only way out of the situation he was in. And I agreed.

As soon as the teams left for work, and while Dubrovskiy was still in bed, I called Vusa aside and, under the guise of the strictest state secret, conveyed everything that my confidant had told me. Vusa's face paled immediately; he doubtless thought of his family, which waited for him after the demobilization, and quietly said:

"That's pretty bold! As a convict, he cares about nothing. He'd as soon bang you on the head and put an end to it. But I've got a family waiting for me, and daddy will soon be back home."

I asked Vusa to keep our conversation between us, and we parted company.

Later, Dubrovskiy walked around the camp with his head down, balefully looking to either side, as if selecting a time and place for his bloody massacre. He happened to be a good psychologist. Two days later, I was sent off to do stockpiling, while he was left behind with the nutcases.

The strongest convicts were selected for stockpiling. It was heavy work, but not dangerous. Over a couple of weeks, all of the timber that had been driven into the impoundment by the weaker convicts, called "perchers," and had been stockpiled on the shore. Preparations began for people to return on foot over the goat trails to the camp center and onward, to the location of a new logging area. We mended, repaired, and rested.

One day it was announced that a dozen of the weakest overworn "perchers" would not walk back, but would be transported by truck to a health-improvement station at the central camp. And based on our friendship, Vusa informed me secretly that I would be sent to the central camp to work there as an agronomist.

"So," I thought, "my letter worked. My wife's doing something."

And a week later, one hundred sixty people, equipped with those same *stezhoks* (used now as ski poles), walked single file, tied with rope into groups of ten for safety, over goat paths to the mountains to fell trees.

My dear Leonid Fedorovich Dubrovskiy, Yuriy Ivanovich Udod, and many others, who became very close to me, will I ever see you again? No, you are not criminals. It is not by accident that you have left a deep fissure in my heart.

15. Departure for a new place

A baker's dozen of us were left on the farm, and that same Vusa remained with us. After his barber departed into the mountains, Vusa again took on a less severe silhouette and began to look human. Now he alone answered for our souls. Yermek, with his parents' permission, took me along to his mud hut. Vusa relocated the "perchers" into my shack. It was tight there, but warm. We awaited the arrival of the trucks to take us away. Our top leadership announced that each of us could leave the farm at any time of day without permission provided we headed east, toward the mountains. We were categorically prohibited from traveling west, where there was an Uigur settlement, or in other remaining directions, and any violator would be considered an escapee. We had no fuel. So many went into the mountains for brushwood, which was abundantly lying around on the shores of the river.

Vusa lived in the farm office. Once he invited me to his place and told me that had saved a bit more than a thousand *karbovanetz*[14] from his pay and wanted to send them to his family. He asked me to go with him to the post office in the village and execute a postal transfer. Of course, I agreed, but I asked to bring our "perchers" along to the village, so that they could stock up on foodstuffs. Otherwise, hey, they are finishing up their "dry ration" and there are no trucks to be heard. Vusa was terribly afraid that his convicts might be caught by some higher-up over there, beyond the limits of the present grounds. He might get chewed out for letting the convicts loose. In the end, though, he agreed. When I told my comrades about this, everyone was happy and began to equip themselves with bags to hold received handouts.

The next morning, our entire team of invalids, under my supervision and that of our warder, traveled to the settlement. At the village itself, Vusa delivered a stern speech and only then let the convicts disperse, ordering them to gather in one hour at "this very place."

Soon, dogs could be heard barking in residential courtyards, while I and Vusa went to the post office. There, we quickly sent the money. Emerging from the post office, Vusa announced he had a toothache, and proposed a visit to the doctor. Once he was inside the doctor's consulting room, I went out onto the small stoop. In the distance, you could hear dogs barking. Apparently, my friends were collecting handouts. I went down the steps and quickly rushed to where the dogs were barking.

On the second floor of one wooden house, I found my guys. They were sitting around a table almost choking on tea, while gathered Uigurs were filling their sacks with

---

[14] Rubles in Ukrainian.

whatever they could share. From there, we proceeded to other houses. We were offered invitations everywhere. Some recognized me from my business.

When bags were filled to overflowing, I formed up my team and led them to "that very place." Vusa was already waiting for us. I gave my report:

"Citizen in charge! All twelve persons, myself the thirteenth, are present. During this expedition there were no serious incidents, except for dogs tearing up the trousers of Ahmet the Chechen."

* * *

About ten days after this excursion, a ton-and-a-half truck arrived for us. As we left, the entire population of the farm turned out in the courtyard. Before boarding the truck, I warmly made my farewells with everyone, as with old friends. Everyone wished me good luck and an early release. And as I sat down Yermek ran up to me and kissed my hand, the hand of a "serious state criminal."

February 1970, Issyk

Order of the
Red Banner

A passenger train approached the Ili railroad station from the north. Sixty convicts, en route to this station in a freight car, worried: "Will the convoy guards from the destination camp come to the station, or must we travel further, to Alma-Ata?" The most experienced convicts knew that one could ride for a long time back and forth along this segment between Alma-Ata and Novosibirsk if, for some reason, the guards didn't show up at the station.

Luckily, the convoy had arrived, and three trucks were standing by to load the prisoners, which meant not having to walk 25 kilometers on foot. Outstanding! And they say there's no camp at the end of the ride but some kind of cushy life: watermelons, tomatoes, and similar food; eat it or push it away. That's what the "blessed south" is all about!

But why are they taking their time loading us into the trucks, and what's in those bags being thrown into them?

We soon find out that packed rations are being loaded, and that we're not going to a watermelon camp but straight out into the mountains — several hundred kilometers from here — on an assignment to float timber down a river. So there's your "stuffed with fruits and vegetables" for you!

A young junior lieutenant who, as it turned out, was commanding the platoon detailed to our assignment, busied himself nearby, and delivered a speech to us before we embarked.

He pointed south, where a steep wall soared high into the sky, of some unknown mountains that many of us were seeing for the first time. He said we were going to be transported over three hundred kilometers to the mountain stream of Chilik. He told us of the beauty that waited for us there.

And how working there wasn't work, but like visiting some kind of spa: a place surrounded by majestic crags, with a mixed forest growing along the shore, teeming with game and wild fruit, while a river of the most pure melted snow flowed below. Gigantic logs floated down the river, and our job was to only walk along and make sure that none of them was cast ashore.

The junior lieutenant did not forget to tell of the wonderful grub that would be received by the future vacationers who listened to him with mouths agape.

We departed along the broken and bumpy road directly to the mountains that could be seen up ahead. Upon approaching very close to them, the trucks turned left, and now the mountains remained steadily to our right, with their snowy caps sparkling in the sun. The view, in fact, was magnificent.

In the evenings we were brought to special "hotels," which is to say "regional jails." We rested there, and set off on the road again in the morning. Although we drove along the plain parallel to the mountains, it felt as if we were steadily going up. Finally, on the third day, we arrived at a mountain valley. In places, it narrowed into gorges. The road rose ever higher and higher until, finally, it arrived at a river flowing through a deep canyon. This was the famous Chilik.

The convicts were divided into two teams that were supposed to keep an eye out for floating logs on the left and right banks. I ended up in the "right bank" team.

The only political convict among the newly arrived "vacationers," I was terribly lonely, and sought someone with whom I could unburden my feelings.

Our first impression of the assignment was not at all like what the junior lieutenant had attempted to portray. The encampment on the river bank painted a pretty bleak picture: several tents occupied by camp administrators and the paramilitary guards were laid out at one end, behind some boulders. On the other side of the boulders a number of dirty gray blankets lay scattered about under the open sky. This is where the "relaxing" prisoners spent the night.

I noticed a person sitting in the shade near one boulder, under a scrap of dirty canvas stretched between scrawny trees, and made my way in his direction.

He was 45 years old, compact, well-fed, tanned, smoothly shaved, and young-looking. A dozen gold teeth sparkled in his mouth. His very elongated face, light and slightly curly hair, and protruding eyes announced that here was a man not from around those parts, more likely a foreigner. We quickly gravitated to each other. It turned out he was a Muscovite serving a long sentence for violating some ordinary article. His job here was that of barber, with an added duty of delivering bread from a neighboring collective farm bakery using pack horses.

He complained that the rains were starting to become overpowering.

"People," he said, indicating the woolen blankets lying around on the ground, "seek shelter from the weather under the nettings, while I hide under a scrap of canvas."

This was Leonid Fedorovich Dubrovskiy, the protagonist of our story.

The tall tale told by the junior lieutenant at the Ili station, about how we would see a vacation resort at Chilik, nevertheless was confirmed in some particulars. Indeed, we were surrounded by an abundance of game and a multitude of different berries. We often saw a hundred mountain goats and wild sheep at a time on the nearby heights. But this "sanative facility" wasn't for us, nor was the game. The paramilitary guards and their favorites filled themselves on plentiful government-issue food and on game, which was often brought to the tents by two soldier-hunters.

The convicts, on the other hand, spent days up to their waists in icy water and exhausted their health. Their strength was melting away, as the food didn't make up for what was used up. They froze in the water by day and they froze under the open sky at night, and they did not recover in time for the next day. Almost every week, one of them would drown in our "vacation" stream.

A good night's rest after a day of exhausting work goes a long way toward recuperating one's strength. For this reason, from the very first days I began to build myself a hut. There was a lot of deadwood along the riverbank, and tall grass grew everywhere. I built a frame out of deadwood, collected grass using a long-handled scythe, and covered my shelter with it. There were days when rain fell incessantly for a day or two, but it didn't matter to me. I was dry and warm and showed up for work with my strength fully recovered.

Dubrovskiy noticed my relatively comfortable digs after one particularly long rain, and began to ask to be invited inside. We came to an agreement. We expanded my hut somewhat, and when we were moved to a new spot, we would build a new hut for two.

It was more cheerful with two of us. Sometimes he would bring some corn meal from the collective farm, and we would cook a marvelous *kisel*[15] with buckthorn berries, which protected against scurvy. With no fresh fruits or vegetables to eat, many complained of scurvy. The *kisel* kept me and Leonid Fedorovich from contracting this dangerous malady. In all, the friendship that grew between us strengthened our position in this singular world.

As I soon found, Leonid Fedorovich was a most marvelous person and likeable storyteller. He felt beauty deeply, understood it, and could forget himself while looking, for example, at the inimitable — as I remember them — sunsets on the Chilik. He paid attention to people, too, even to some common criminals who had attracted his attention, and rendered keen descriptions. In each one, he first saw a person and tried to understand how the person had become who he was, and in what environment he was formed.

He knew his own worth. He said that nature had not shortchanged him in either intelligence or talent, and complained that he could not use these gifts, exhausting

---

[15] Hot stewed fruit thickened with starch.

them on trifles, instead. For some reason he was greatly afraid of getting lost in our world, like a grain of sand. He even was afraid to die without having left any memory in this world of there having lived, at one time, at some place, a certain Leonid Fedorovich Dubrovskiy.

Late in the evening, after we had settled in to sleep and the chirping of the grasshoppers masked conversation, he would tell me of his previous life, asking me to remember what he was telling me, so that someday — he placed his hopes on me, for some reason — I could write it down and get all of this across to future generations. Where is Leonid Fedorovich today? Is he alive? I've heard nothing of him since. Still, after a quarter of a century, I am fulfilling his request. Our further narrative will presently proceed on his behalf.

We had just eaten supper. Rain started to sprinkle. Leonid Fedorovich and I climbed into our hut. It was apparent that it had rained the day before in the upper reaches of the river, as clouds appeared in the distance, lightning flashed but no thunder could be heard, as it was too far away. Warm rain melted the glaciers somewhat, and now the river was rampaging and roaring. For a long time, I could not get used to the incessant noise. And when one of us would die, I could not fall asleep for a long time. I would cover my head. Then the rush of the river seemed to me to be the hissing of a cold snake that was trying to slither into my bed.

Leonid Fedorovich became used to this rumble.

"You call this water? You think it's too loud? You should have seen what this river was up to in the second half of July and the first half of August. Now there was one wild animal! We would sometimes lose three people in a week. Now? It's not a torrent, but a trickle."

But I kept listening attentively to the river's bellow, so in an apparent attempt to distract me from it, Leonid Fedorovich asked,

"What is your view on heredity?"

The question took me completely by surprise. Not knowing the reason it was asked, I said,

"Heredity." I pronounced the word slowly, trying to impart some science to my response. "Heredity is the transmission, via chromosomes or genes — whatever you want to call them — of external and internal individualities from parents to their children. For example, hair color, eye color, manner of walking, or formal resemblance. Cases are known where entire families consist of talented musicians, mathematicians, and so on."

"My father," I continued, "was educated as a medical man and worked for a long time in one place. So when some young patient he had never seen before would come to him, he would peer at him and say,

'You, apparently, are of the such-and-such family?' he'd ask, and he was never mistaken."

Then I wanted to use various examples to show how parental attributes are transmitted by heredity to offspring but, as I recalled Mendel, Darwin, and Morgan, I realized this would take quite a bit of time. I abruptly descended from the clouds of science back to Leonid Fedorovich, and asked him:

"Why is this of interest to you?"

"Well, you see," he said, "I've been interested in this subject a long time. I am a man with no heredity. I never had a father, or a mother, or any grandparents."

"What are you trying to say — that you sprang from sea foam?" I asked him.

"Almost, yes. The sea apparently played an important part in my appearance in this world, at least."

"One summer morning, a bundle was found on the front steps of the orphanage in Yevpatoria. When the nannies opened the bundle, they found a boy, wrapped in expensive diapers and a silk blanket. A note had been pressed into the infant's right hand. There, in a steady feminine hand, was written, "Leonid Dubrovskiy, born May 15, 1901, baptized."

"That, unfortunately," continued Leonid Fedorovich, "was your humble servant. Ever since, the question 'Who are my parents?' never left me as I grew up. Yevpatoria is a resort city, there are palaces all around. In summer, the famous Yevpatoria sea beach would fill with elegant people from Petersburg — princes and counts and the deskbound nobility. That's where the beginnings of Leonid Dubrovskiy were deposited. Love, apparently, was not durable, and by the following year my grandmother — at least, that's who I think it was — brought her daughter to Yevpatoria under the pretext of urgent treatment, to the old place, far away from the malicious tongues of Petersburg. Here, after the daughter acquired what one might call a marketable condition, she was taken back, after having first cruelly determined the future of her grandson. I am certain that's what happened, as the orphanage of the Holy Virgin

Mary in Yevpatoria was a special asylum for just such children."

Forty-four years had passed since Dubrovskiy came into this world. However, having told me the story of his appearance, he started to fret; I could hear him sobbing.

I started to feel sorry for him. Every living thing is drawn to its mother, seeking love and affection. But there was no such affection or parental love for the gentle, surprisingly sensitive Leonid Fedorovich.

"Don't think," said Leonid Fedorovich to me after a few days, "that I am proud of my high ancestry. It was just an assumption about my parents. From my earliest childhood, however, this assumption aroused an aversion, a burning hatred for representatives of high society. I always loved ordinary people, working people. I took my patronymic from my adoptive father, Feodor, a Ukrainian farmer in the Crimea. You see, we were cared for at the orphanage until we were seven; then the administration set out to find farming families and concluded agreements to place children for an upbringing that included work. So it was that in 1908, Feodor Ivanovich Fesenko, a Ukrainian farmer, took in four fosterlings from the orphanage (two boys and two girls) and brought them up in Aktachi, a large village on the shores of Lake Sasyk. Under the agreement, the orphanage made a payment for us to our foster parents. So we stepbrothers and stepsisters spent four years with our adoptive parents, whom we remember with the warmest of recollections. We participated in all agricultural work with them, and at the same time attended an elementary four-grade school.

When we returned to the orphanage, invited teachers prepared us to enter special intermediate educational institutions. The orphanage was a privileged institution. In addition to government funds, it received a lot of subsidies from notable people in the form of gifts (some, apparently, felt pangs of conscience). And so, the orphanage had money, and they cared for their charges until they had received an appropriate education.

In 1913, I entered the Yevpatoria "real school"[16]. I wanted to later attend the university, but this school did not award diplomas, and without one there would be no attending any university. While at this school, I selected the specialization "commerce" at the suggestion of my orphanage teachers (we never broke our relationship with the orphanage for long). Upon completing this school, in 1916, the same orphanage arranged for me to enter the Kiev Institute of Commerce and study there for a year and a half.

In spring of 1918, when Kiev was occupied by the Germans and Hetman Skoropadskiy was in charge, I dragged myself, a seventeen-year-old jack-a-dandy at the time, out of there back to my native Crimea. I'll tell you that, as a typical representative of the insulted and humiliated masses, I put my whole soul behind the Bolsheviks from the start of the revolution. But it was even worse in Crimea than in Ukraine. There were Tatar nationalists and Russian monarchists operating there. I fled to the partisans and acquired the military specialty of

---

[16] A type of secondary school that stressed vocational skills.

machine-gunner. In the stone quarries around Yevpatoria, where the partisans hid, I received my first baptism of fire. The revolution gave me wings. Later, behind the trigger of a machine gun, I mowed down the enemies of Soviet power on various fronts, avenging my downtrodden youth and standing for the establishment of sublime truth on Earth.

In 1920, for active duty in combat and exhibiting heroism during the liberation of Crimea from Wrangel's forces, I was awarded the Order of the Red Banner.

The civil war came to an end. The cannons fell silent, and the machine guns stuttered to a stop. Demobilization began. The country returned to peacetime labor. Conquering heroes began to appear in every city and village of our great land. Some, the least assertive, went off to the hamlets of their families and began to "fix" agriculture; or went into cities to bring plants and factories back from the ashes. Others, who represented that Russian *volniytsa*[17] for which our Mother Russia has been famous from old times, laid claim to a warmer place under the sun. Energetic and undisciplined, they had adopted the slogan "Beat and crush the class enemies!" back in the army and now, in peacetime, they declared themselves to be arch-revolutionaries, forcing themselves into power in district and *volost*[18] councils, personally engaging in beating and crushing — under the pretext of consolidating Soviet power — not just class enemies but peasants and the intelligentsia as well, thus sowing discontent all around

---

[17] Daredevils, outlaws

[18] Rural county

themselves. No sooner had the battles of the Civil War ended than "Green" bands appeared in the forests and mountains, often made up of those who had recently worn a *budenovka*[19]. These were also dissatisfied.

Meanwhile, the arch-revolutionaries, in demonstrating irrepressible vigilance toward others, did not forget about themselves. They took up residence in merchant houses and married merchant daughters. They surrounded themselves with rugs, expensive furniture, arms, horses, automobiles, and drunkenness. Red Army men guarded their apartments and property. Eventually, the news of their behavior reached Moscow, and usually a firing squad would put an end to the whole thing.

I did not go down either of those two paths. First of all, I had nobody to return to. While the war was going on, I had felt the elbows of my brothers-in-arms. When the war ended and we all crept back to our homes, I felt a terrible loneliness. In the war, I had thrown myself headfirst into this heroic battle. I forgot about myself. But now, I had to think for a while about my own future.

At that time, our unit was stationed in the city of Tsaritsyn. Tall, well-proportioned, and young (in my twentieth year), dressed in red breeches and wearing an Order of the Red Banner on my chest, I made a seductive impression on the young ladies of Tsaritsyn. To be frank, not only did those young representatives of the fair sex simply pursue me, but so did their mothers and fathers. These, customarily of the "have-beens," charmed me not only with the beauty of their daughters but with their

---

[19] Pointed Red Army hat with earflaps.

surviving hidden gold assets, at which they only hinted. By right of kinship, I could have designs on these assets.

To make a long story short, as a twenty-year-old fellow, I married one merchant's daughter and received a not insubstantial dowry.

If you only knew the kind of a wedding that was arranged! It was a of mix of the old and new. On my side, my comrades-in-arms were present in their red breeches, strapped tightly, well-heeled, with red banners all around that had been borrowed from our unit; on the other, coddled young ladies in silks and pearls sat with their stout papas and mamas at tables groaning with viands and expensive wines. All around, there were classy furniture items, rugs, paintings.

Immediately after the wedding, our parents intentionally moved into a small outbuilding, which stood right there in the yard, while we youngsters remained in the big house with old servants. When authorities were requisitioning the houses of the local bourgeoisie, my Order of the Red Banner began to act as a peculiar taboo: the special expropriation committees didn't even stop by the *podvoriye*[20] where I lived with my young wife.

Of course, I understood the whole ridiculous situation I had become part of in connection with the marriage, and it weighed on me. In 1922, being demobilized, I moved to Moscow with my wife, to get away from my kin, who with all their machinations used me as a shield behind which to hide.

---

[20] Suburban household.

Moscow — fabulous city of white stone! I had a private apartment of seven rooms, a pair of parade horses, and a driver, while the wife had a chambermaid and a cook. Everything was in grand style, as in the old days. But why shouldn't a Red commander, not to mention one who wore an Order, have such "juice"? There weren't many Order-wearers, then. They were greatly esteemed. This "juice" had two sources: the assets of my in-laws, on the one hand, and being an Order-wearing victor, on the other. They somehow complemented each other. You wouldn't get far with just an Order without money. In those days, it was easy to set oneself up somewhere in a warm little corner in a Soviet institution, but one didn't want to lose one's freedom and independence. I was still a businessman by education, though the country was in such a deplorable state that thinking of business was out of the question.

Still, some people thought about it. The Soviet authorities announced a New Economic Program (NEP). Lenin advised us to learn from the same bourgeoisie whose heads we had been lopping off only a couple of years before. Private capital was given a green light.

The "have-beens," whose ranks had thinned considerably by that time, came around slowly to this new Leninist idea. Some kind of hope nonetheless took root: the Soviet authorities wanted to learn something from them. Was that right? Won't this be just more dirty pool? They assembled, and organized themselves, so as not to operate as individuals in the new commerce but collectively, and they fetched their assets from hidey-holes and tallied them up. It's good to be part of a company. But the old and familiar names of the "have-beens" affronted the ears of the new, Soviet man-on-the-street, who had fought and spilled his proletarian blood fighting against them.

Later, if you recall, the ranks of the "have-beens" were thrown into some kind of panic by the so-called "working opposition," led by the then-prominent Shlyapnikov, who saw in the New Economic Program a restoration of capitalism in a country that had just eliminated that same capitalism.

"It would be good if some kind of red banner, even threadbare, could be found for such a company. With the color red, things would be calmer for capital as well," crossed the minds of many former businessmen.

From the earliest times, the Moscow fat cats had strong ties to all corners of our immense country. They quietly found out, through their Tsaritsyn wheeler-dealers, that right under their noses was what they so wanted to have: a young, healthy Order-wearer who, by the way, was a businessman by education. You have guessed that they were talking about your obedient servant.

My Order of the Red Banner had assumed some kind of magical significance in my life.

Soon, I stood at the head of the company of all Moscow restaurants and cabarets. At that time, this was a most enormous enterprise, with about ten thousand workers and employees. A thousand artists and musicians alone worked at our locations. This was a most profitable business. Soviet gold poured into my partners' pockets.

You might ask, why didn't I become a part of the Soviet commercial machine, why did I again find myself among the "have-beens"?

In this case, everything was proceeding according to Lenin. As I said, Lenin encouraged learning about business. At the time, Soviet commerce amounted to the buzzing of mosquitoes. If I had gone that route, I would have had to become a student, but as a businessman, I could have — and should have — been a teacher of that which Vladimir Ilyich was exhorting us to undertake. My conscience is clear in this matter.

With that, Leonid Fedorovich fell silent, as it was a very late hour.

* * *

"So, where did we stop last time?" That was the question with which Leonid Fedorovich normally began his narrative.

"Moscow. You were the head of 'Dubrovskiy and Company'."

"Yes, yes! The most interesting period. It was, you might say, a period of ascendancy in my life. Afterward, everything would slide down a ramp to this damned Chilik!

So, back then, we in the company were growing fabulously rich. My Order continued to be a magical amulet. In the struggle with various private competitors, I would nip them in the bud with my position as a Red: relevant Soviet institutions simply wouldn't let them get under way. And I won't hide the fact that "gifts" to relevant persons "for their efforts" played some role. That's on my conscience.

Imagine my place of business in Moscow. It was a marvelous two-story building with columns, where all the rooms were filled with clerks of both sexes. My office on the second floor sat behind a massive double door, upholstered with sound-absorbing material. Inside, on the walls, there was a huge portrait of Lenin with his closest associates. And there, behind a desk as massive as the doors, sat your obedient servant with that same Order of the Red Banner on his chest. Introducing themselves, representatives of financial institutions immediately became diminutive and acquiescent.

Within a very short time of Lenin's call for the New Economic Policy, my company established what the Marxists call a "solid basis" for itself.

Apropos, I'll mention that the Soviet gold that tumbled in heaps into our pockets did not come from laborers. So I'll tell you frankly, we were not exploiters.

As a rule, we paid our workers and employees double — sometimes triple — the going rate, depending on the job, as compared to the same work at government enterprises. Our clerical workers were paid very high salaries, even if they weren't our partners, as were persons who dealt with tangible assets. And none of them ever engaged in any embezzlement or theft.

Our profits poured from the nepmen[21], who we sheared like sheep. Our restaurants were too expensive for working people. Based on wages paid in those days, we were completely out of their league.

---

[21] Businessmen who operated under the New Economic Program

Corpulent nepmen with their profligate sons and expensive mistresses, various accomplished grifters from the families of former princes and counts, and the entire motley elite of those years gathered around our numerous small tables, hungry for the easy score.

It was at those tables that transactions with lots of zeros were made and partners entered into business deals. It was here that connections were cemented and family ties were established.

It was for this non-laboring public that we attempted to create an environment that enabled us to pump the greatest amount of money out of them: various seductive inducements, private trysting rooms, cabarets with half-naked girls, casinos with svelte croupiers in tuxedos and well-groomed dames.

And so, on such a basis — which the Dubrovskiy company commanded — there arose, to use the same language, a corresponding superstructure. Every partner came to have a luxury apartment with period furniture, suits were ordered from the best foreign tailors, they had their personal carriages, and they spent entire summers on the Black Sea coast. And there, there would be new meetings, trysts, and love. It seemed it would never end.

Unfortunately, this life in paradise was temporary. It is known that Lenin introduced the New Economic Policy in all seriousness and permanently. But Lenin soon died. After his death, his associates began feuding. Each of them, as you know, wanted to demonstrate his rightness, his interpretation of Lenin's precepts. By the way, by the end of the twenties, the economic situation in our country had improved significantly. Lenin had not erred: the stores were full of goods, and the situation with bread was as it had been under the old regime. The nepmen had done much. True, there was still much they had not been able to accomplish. Soviet businessmen weren't given enough time to learn their trade, as authorities began to squeeze their teachers in every way with a new system of taxes.

Gradually, the opponents of Lenin's New Economic Policy gained the upper hand in the Kremlin. It seemed to many hotheads, who had little real-world experience, that all they needed to do is put their hand to industry and business and everything would proceed smoothly. They thought, "Hey, our advantage over our blind competition is that we *plan*!"

This entire substitution of one economic policy with another was done gradually, without evicting the expropriators, as if nothing new was going on, but business life was dealt an unrecoverable blow. The economy, which had been gaining strength, began to fall. Lines a kilometer long began to appear at stores.

Company taxes became so high that a situation came about in which private companies first curtailed their activities, and later closed completely.

In order to hang on somehow, many nepmen tried to hide their income. And as always in such circumstances, they tried to grease the palms of employees in financial institutions. Maybe you recall the trials, in Moscow and Leningrad, of the financial workers and nepmen who took and offered bribes?

Our clientele noticeably shrank as well because of this "assault" on private capital. But our profits were tolerable.

We could still live. At that time, the "assault" was directed at private businesses that manufactured goods. Businesses in the service sector, such as our restaurants, retained their earlier Leninist position.

This grace period, however, did not last long. The "assault" began there, too. The magical influence of my Order gradually diminished. We started to pay more in taxes than we received in income. We began to lose our original capital, and there arose the danger that if we, contrary to common sense, continued to hold on to our business, we would end up as beggars. For this reason, we soon dissolved the company.

At almost the same time, an "assault" began against our lesser brother, the private farmer. His fate was worse than ours. Bled dry, he was literally dying off. It was as though the government has opened foreign-currency stores in the cities for our salvation, filled with various goods. And we, the former people of the business world, who had hoarded something of our bygone assets, lived sheltered lives during those years that were most severe in terms of food, not forgetting to travel each summer (as was our established habit) to the blessed Black Sea to Crimea. But a fellow who, having clung to his property and having paid with his last grain to satisfy the demands of the authorities who were throwing him into the street, would finally rush to a last refuge and leave for the city. And if he could not understand the adopted policy, the so-called "general" line, he would in most cases die, since his access to foreign-currency stores was, for completely understandable reasons, barred.

But assets belonging to people of our kind were melting away, too. Something had to be undertaken.

To begin with, I got rid of my private apartment and carriage, fired the servants, and used the privileges of an Order-wearer to obtain an apartment in a government house on Bolshaya Polyanka in that same Moscow, populated with various former military ranks of distinction. I still had the "juice": I dressed only in suits of foreign cloth and tailoring, with a raccoon fur coat and hat, and the whole getup was decorated with that same Order of the Red Banner. Now, when I visited the Black Sea coast, I passed myself off not as a nepman, but as a director of some anonymous Moscow factory. I changed my colors somewhat. When I met the "have-beens," I pretended not to recognize them.

I needed to find some business that would bring income under the new conditions. I somehow found out that in Leningrad the "offensive" did not affect barbers. At the time, I knew nothing of this occupation, considering it to be menial, but I traveled there.

The message was confirmed: petty proprietors of the hairdressing salons were still flourishing and even believed the "offensive" would not touch them.

I decided to act. But now I acted independently, neither participating in or organizing any companies. Here, my Order played a positive role many times: I was permitted to open a hairdressing business.

On Sadovaya Street, ever since the times of the revolutionary battles, there was a run-down commercial building. I rented it, repaired it, and set up fifty barbers in two enormous halls, one for men and the other for women.

Everything was going well: the business was quite profitable.

But then they introduced new rules: barber shops with a staff of fifty employees paid so much, those with twenty-five paid less, and so on, with the most minuscule establishments paying only pennies. I immediately laid off half of my employees, and even made my wife the cashier. But even so, they managed to throw you out into the street. The situation had become critical. I didn't even recoup what I had spent to repair the salon.

I decided to acquire a profession. In the men's room I set up a barbering station and on the peak days (normally Saturday afternoon) I put on a snow-white work coat and unusually massive horn-rimmed glasses, went out to the waiting room, and selected a victim who, from a look at his clothes, was not well off. I had the appearance not of a barber, but of some medical doctor. I invited the chosen one with a commanding gesture:

"If you please!" I would say, politely pointing to the salon.

The victim becomes confused and wants to say it's not his turn. But my authoritative "if you please" makes him stand, and he enters the salon. There, I begin to experiment with him. If during the session the victim begins to cringe, I explain that I am doing all of this at no charge, out of my respect for the working class.

It didn't always go smoothly for me. I recall how, on a successive Saturday, I invited a mud-bespattered old geezer and began to work on him. If you only knew how much unpleasantness he caused me, especially after I was careless enough to tell him that I was doing all this for him at absolutely no charge. He then became completely enraged. The whole operation ended with my apologizing to him, after which I invited my best barber, and he perfunctorily corrected my tonsorial hocus-pocus.

Afterward, I learned that this old fellow was the chief engineer of the neighboring factory. That's what you get for judging people by their clothes!

The incident with the geezer that I told you about yesterday didn't force me to give up my experiments. On the contrary. Now, I would daily — not just on peak days — don a snow-white work coat, enter the waiting room, and honestly announce:

"Whoever would like to voluntarily undergo a free session, please enter."

Volunteers were found. Later, some of them became long-time permanent models, as for a painter. Unlike a painter's models, I didn't pay them, but before a session, I would call the next volunteer into my office and treat them to a large glass of some kind of multi-star brandy and some chasers, after which he would be entirely at my disposal.

I quickly picked up the skills of the hairdressing business and soon was shaving and cutting hair as well as the other barbers. It became obvious to me that this menial occupation was not so complicated. The attendant at the bath who soaps your back, or the manicurist who works on your nails, or the masseur who massages your mulchy body, and many similar occupations — all of these are lackeys, and to this day, I wholeheartedly despise this kind of human activity.

But I was captivated by another side of this business. Do you recall Leskov's story *The Toupée Master*? Well I, just as that master, was carried away by the idea of the unity of form and "content." I began to look not only at the client's physiognomy but also to peek into his soul. I became a psychologist and began to seek the true language of the toupée art. Before starting to work on the next client, I spoke with him. An image formed quickly in my head, and I then tried to embody it using barber's tools, just as a painter would use brushes and paints. In addition to the usual services of a barber, I began to consult with my clients on what became them and what didn't. Later I equipped a photography laboratory in the salon and photographed the typical features of my clientele. Using these photos, I compiled an enormous album of client specimen types. I also acquired hundreds of photographs of famous people, and my customers used these to choose their hair style. Subsequently, on Leningrad streets, you could encounter personalities who had, over several sessions, made themselves look like the composer Skryabin (moustache turned slightly upward, pointed goatee), the military pilot-hero Serov, Voroshilov, and Kalinin. A number of Yesenins and Mayakovskys walked around the city as well.

I attentively peered at arriving clients and then only announced that I could make them look like this or that number (referring to the numbers of the photographs in my albums) and that I could not do that for some other number, as it was unbecoming.

There were daredevils who wanted to look like Stalin. But I didn't want to undertake such a likeness, lest something bad happen. Only now, here in the camps —

With a Red guerilla's card, I traveled on the city's streetcars for free and the card let me bypass the line waiting to receive bread in grocery stores. In the House of Party Education, there hung, among others, a portrait of the Red guerilla L. F. Dubrovskiy. My Order came in very handy. I was elected to the city Soviet and was invited to various gatherings where I related my heroic achievements during the revolution. All of my appearances were met with thunderous applause.

On one city street, I rented a small building and opened my artistic hairdressing salon there (that's what it said on the sign, too). I didn't chase after clients. I had money, and in my salon, I refined my art on a selected public.

Everything was going well. Nobody disturbed me. Several years passed after Leningrad. Over time, apparently, everything was forgotten and I, frankly, was drawn to Moscow.

There was nothing particular in Moscow to gladden me: neglect was everywhere, the store shelves were bare, and lines were a kilometer long. The police roved the streets of Moscow, hunting suspicious Muscovites and hauling them off "to ascertain identity," later sending them (with coded designations of either "SD-5" or "SH-5") in troop trains east, to Siberia. The meaning of the code was revealed only after arrival. "SD-5" meant socially dangerous, with 5 years of imprisonment; "SH-5" meant socially harmful, with the same five years in the camps. This was how Moscow was cleansed of "non-labor elements." But heaven spared me. Then again, I was even afraid to go out into the street without my Order, and it, apparently, rescued me. In because they can't put me any further away, or for any longer — as you see, I maintain such a terrifying image for our warden, Vusa, that the convicts are spooked.

Rumors about me spread throughout Leningrad. I was overwhelmed with clients from the worlds of science and art. The municipal utility office organized a photographic exhibition of my work. Later, competitions were held among barbers. The jury voted me the best artistic barber in Leningrad. Photographs of my work were exhibited in hairdressing salons in Leningrad and Moscow and became examples for emulation.

In the eyes of the 'authorities,' however, my toupée art was merely a hobby. For the financial bodies, I was the last of the nepman Mohicans, holding on somehow either because of my Order or because of this very artistry that I've been talking about. In the mid-1930s, I was taxed so heavily that, together with my wife, I quietly slipped out of Leningrad, leaving behind all my output to cover employee salaries and taxes.

In Moscow, I left my wife in the apartment that we still kept on Bolshaya Polyanka. As for myself, I covered my tracks and took off for my native Crimea and settled down in Yevpatoria.

There, I was my own man. Before long, the Yevpatoria society of Red guerillas accepted me in their organization. They did not have to make any inquiries along those lines, because there were people still alive alongside whom I fought against the Whites.

all fairness, I had to work. Before long, I opened a hairdressing parlor at the Leningradsky Rail Terminal, with the permission of the station's administration.

My earnings weren't bad, something one could live on, in those anxious times when everyone prayed in the morning — unless they'd been "picked up" the night before. Then again, they were "removing" mostly the important and distinguished people. Sometimes I even entertained the thought of whether I should ditch my Order, of whether it could cause misfortune. It was a lot safer to be one of the little people. At least nobody made "enemies of the people" out of them or arranged trial proceedings; they weren't scoffed at as much. And even if such a nobody was caught in order "to ascertain identity," that person would, like a small fish, be thrown into the next train and sent without fuss to the East.

Again, all of this passed me by. Just in case I acquired various (though phony) documents attesting to my socially valuable activities. And I still carried my red partisan's book in my jacket pocket in such a way that half of it stuck out. The only thing I did not change was my appearance: in winter I solemnly went about in that same raccoon, carrying the most gigantic monogrammed leather briefcase of English manufacture in my hands.

The clientele at the station was terribly impermanent, and I turned into an ordinary working barber. I said no kind word to anyone, nor did I hear any. However big a genius a client might be, having seen me for the first and very likely the last time in his life, he could not evaluate my work after one visit. I will say frankly that I began to suffer in my work at the station. Life became gray and uninteresting.

Life was passing by, but I still wanted to soar, to hear some of that sweet music.

Sometimes I met with my former companions, who complained of various vexations. They undertook many things in secret and walked around daily in fear of discovery and arrest. Among other things, from their conversations with one shrewd operator in illegal commerce, I learned that one could earn tons of money — under the counter, naturally — selling foreign music records.

The big question was how to get them.

As I've mentioned, I was fed up with the hairdressing business and its minuscule earnings. I decided to change my business to records.

But if I'm going to do something, I like to do it all the way, on a grand scale. First of all, I thoroughly studied this new subject and ascertained that there really was a big demand for foreign records.

I got in touch with some workers at the Ministry of Foreign Affairs and through them, on a mutually beneficial basis, began to receive the requisite goods. The diplomatic mail started to indirectly work for me as well.

At first, I established ties with the Gramplastinka [22] department manager of one large second-hand commission shop. Later, as goods arrived from abroad, I would systematically deliver packages to him in a cab. They were brought into a salable state in the department and

---

[22] "Grammophone Record" brand name.

appropriate batches were packaged, intended for a single buyer. A list of records was also written out by hand.

In the morning, after a substantial breakfast I would, if it was winter, don my raccoon fur and go off, as if on important government business, to the commission store. There, my briefcase, with the goods inside, would be brought out from under the counter, and I would start to mix with the many customers of the Gramplastinka department. My eye was experienced enough to determine whether to offer my product to this or that customer.

Having selected a victim that merited my trust, I would apologize and from the altitude of my raccoon fur and my dozen shining golden teeth, I would profess that I was an admirer of foreign records and that I had brought along something to the store to sell on commission.

"Would you like to see my little list?" I would offer.

My victim, of course, would agree and after a short conversation, would hand me a large sum, satisfied with this chance and favorable bargain. I, on the other hand, would retire to the closest restaurant to dine after such righteous labors. During that time, another batch with a new list would be prepared in the Gramplastinka department.

The Gramplastinka department had a lot of its own merchandise, and the accommodating salesmen would mawkishly offer customers records with the songs of the composer Dunayevsky, performances by people's songstress Kovalyova, and speeches of comrade Stalin. Customers were turned off by these, and I was a lucky find for them.

Jazz was becoming popular at that time. In every possible way, our press was inveighing against this bourgeois music of the stagnating West. And there was a great demand expressly for jazz. What a pity that I could not fully satisfy it. But commerce was lively.

True, I sometimes experienced acute conflicts while selling records, and I worried a lot. But I got away with it for several years, and materially, I lived in clover.

Let me tell you a story. I asked for some kind of insolently fabulous amount from this one general who had come to the commission store to buy foreign records. He didn't have that kind of money on his person, so he proposed that I ride with him to his general's apartment in his car that, as I understood from his gesture, stood not far away. He even promised, out of kindness, to drop me off later at my apartment.

The general's suggestion was so direct that I couldn't refuse, as I feared to arouse a suspicion that I was afraid of something.

Can you imagine what thoughts passed through my head during this ride with the general in his car? So we set off, and I figure it out: we're going directly to the Fifth Police Division with the goods, the material evidence. No, we've gone past. Apparently, they're taking me to the Police Directorate. Maybe that's where the general works. But fortunately, we pass by the Directorate as well. Soon after, we stop next to the house where the general lives. A great weight lifts from my soul.

The general invites me into his apartment. There in the vestibule, I removed my raccoon and then the general introduced me, dressed in my marvelous English suit and leggings and wearing my Order of the Red Banner, to his wife. The missus was happy with her husband's acquisition. Apropos, lunch was ready, and I was invited to sit at the table. Three sheets to the wind, the general and I recalled the military days of the civil war and even movingly shed sweet tears over the fact that those awful days were behind us and we could now even interest ourselves with foreign records.

After lunch, the same soldier chauffeur dropped me off at Bolshaya Polyanka with a heavy billfold.

In the Gramplastinka department, everyone truly suffered a fright when they saw me being led out into the street by the general. The next day, I explained everything to them, and our business continued.

The world turns. Life goes on. But our human existence, how short it is! Despite everything, I followed my old habit and traveled to the Black Sea coast every summer.

As I have already said, there I pretended to be a relaxing director of some anonymous factory. Decked out in brand new clothes, with the same permanent Order (and young to boot), I made an indelible impression on the female visitors.

That year, I met a black-eyed woman journalist there. Oh, how we fell in love with each other, how we fell in love! Time passed imperceptibly. It was already time to head homeward, but we kept putting off the end to these most happy days of our lives. She took delight in my sharp intellect and technical knowledge (although between us, at that time I could only shine in my knowledge of my repertoire of foreign records). In short, I pulled the wool over her eyes.

There was this time we were coming back from another outing in an overcrowded streetcar (this happened in Yalta). Standing, we hung from the straps, feasting our eyes on each other. Our last days in Crimea! Soon, we would go our separate ways.

I noticed two antediluvian geezers sitting in our compartment. I recognized one of them. He was from Yevpatoria. These folks should have died long before, but apparently, still came for treatments. So the one from Yevpatoria looks at me, then again, and finally starts speaking:

"Leonid Fedorovich, is that you? Howdy do! It's been ages since we've seen one another!"

But noticing that I don't want to talk with him, he continued the conversation, only this time he spoke to his companion:

"That's our barber from Yevpatoria. An artist! The man's got golden hands. Oh, how he shaved us, how he cut our hair, and later, he took off somewhere..."

I was ready to kill this fossil, but at this point, the streetcar arrived at a stop. And although we needed to travel on for quite a way, I took my love by the hand and dragged her out the exit. There, on solid ground again, I took my lady friend by the arm and said to her, as if I were about to be put to death:

"Well, did you hear? Do you understand who I am? Will you continue to love a 'bah-bah'?" (I deliberately stressed and distorted the last word.)

She was rattled. But coming around somewhat, she announced that the important thing about love wasn't social position or one's job... and all sorts of similar thoughts.

I'll tell you frankly, though, after this episode, the fire went out of our love as if a wind had blown it out. True, she'd still sweet-talk me when we met, but I consciously pursued a breakup.

That fall, dejected by my failure in love, I returned to Moscow. This was in 1937. Reports on the trials never left the front page. Prosecutor General Vyshinsky [23] raged. Most of the time, however, even this kind of a prefabricated "open due process" wasn't available, since a special meeting with the NKVD without any kind of trial, with no skimping, foisted a five-year term on its victims and sent them off to a corresponding "rest home." And nevertheless, despite the terrible danger, many funny stories circulated around the country. There was the one about how one night, several strangers barged into the apartment of one senior official. At first, the occupants were scared to death, but soon they rejoiced, because the intruders were ordinary robbers and not NKVD agents. The apartment dwellers had never before so hospitably received such people as they did that night, and the robbers were barely able to carry away what the occupants freely gave to them.

---

[23] Andrey Janevich Vyshinsky (1883-1954) - Prosecutor General of the USSR (1935-1939), the legal mastermind of Joseph Stalin's Great Purge.

I received the grace of God in those terrible years, as well. Before, it had seemed that my Order, which flashed on my chest, kept saving me, but by this time, Orders had tarnished. Every morning, news would spread through the apartments that this one or that one had been "taken" among distinguished people, many of whom wore Orders or were Party members. "But these," I told myself, trying to stay calm, "are 'enemies of the people' and politicians. What do I have to do with them?"

During my absence from Moscow, the ranks of the diplomatic post office of the Ministry of Foreign Affairs had thinned, particularly among those of its representatives through whose channels I received foreign records. The branch upon which I had so comfortably nestled had been sawn off at its very root.

I had to find honest labor, so I started to follow the announcements in *Evening Moscow*. And somehow, in one of the issues, I see: "such-and-such plant needs an experienced barber," so I decided to go there the next day.

Again, with the same fur coat and the same briefcase, filled with papers and photos attesting to my high skills, I got off the streetcar and set off for the plant entrance. Near the plant gates, I was met by a presentably dressed, middle-aged man, most probably an engineer. He asks me:

"Are you here to visit us?" and without giving me a chance to reply, he continues: "Let's go!"

Skipping the check point, he led me directly to the plant director's office. I don't understand. Why am I receiving such attention? But I go.

In the antechamber there's a giant with a beard and striped pants. I gave him my hat and fur coat, and then my escort leads me to a door covered in black imitation leather cloth, with a small mirrored sign on it that reads "Director." Bypassing the procession of those waiting in the director's anteroom, my escort opens the door. Past the door I walk, like a wind-up doll, along a carpeted path to a huge desk, behind which sits a huge man with a bald head. He immediately rose from his massive oak chair and extended a meaty paw across the table to me.

"Sit down!" he said, indicating a chair, identical to his own, that stood at the table. He remained standing.

"Oh, am I sunk!" I thought to myself. "Who do they think I am?"

But there was nothing to be done. I sat down. For the first time in my life, my Order burned on my chest. I wanted to cover it with my briefcase. But it, too, made of yellow imported English leather, incited envy in people. I'll admit, for the first time in my life, I lost my bearings. But the director remained standing.

Finally, with shaking hands, I took my copy of *Evening Moscow* out of my briefcase, showed it to the director, and in a sepulchral voice that was not my own asked:

"Is it you that needs a barber?"

Not expecting such a question, the director plonked his sizeable body down into his chair. "Well," I'm thinking, "now I'm in for it." But he recovered quickly and started to look at my various diplomas and photographs, which attested to my servile specialty. Then he proposed that I look at an empty room that was right next to the office and intended to be a barber shop.

When we came out into the front room, the attendant came to a point and kept his eyes on us until we entered the future barber shop. The door remained half-open behind us, and soon the attendant stuck in his cloddish head, trying apparently to figure out what the big people were up to.

Meanwhile, I was walking around the room and was saying to the director:

"We'll put a mirror here, that thing there, and that other thing someplace else, arrange the lights like so," and so on.

Apparently, the attendant figured it out, because when I soon returned from the director's office and demanded my clothing, this idiot suddenly starts talking:

"Oh, you and I will get along fine; me, here, and you, there," he said, pointing at the neighboring room.

I didn't say a word. After he had given me my hat and coat, I took out my wallet and gave this lackey a fiver "for his trouble." Gold may be easily told, buddy.

At that moment, a middle-aged man with a briefcase came in from outside and immediately headed into the director's office. A murmur went around the room: this was the ministry representative that management had been waiting for.

Nonplussed, I never returned to that plant. I hoarded my Order away, began to dress more plainly, and soon found work as a barber, only at a different plant.

Life became gray and uninteresting. I worked like that until the war, and lived primarily on my old savings.

As I've said before, I lived on Bolshaya Polyanka in Moscow. One of my neighbors was an interesting old fellow, a Don Cossack named Feodor Vasilyevich[24] (and as he spoke the old man's name and patronymic, Leonid Federovich began to whisper, truly afraid that someone would overhear us). So this very same Feodor Vasilyevich, a well-known designer of Russian semiautomatic weapons, would sometimes say the following to me with tears in his eyes, not long before the war:

"Where are we headed, Leonid Fedorovich? We have good weapons, good soldiers, and we had good military leaders. And all this is good in skillful hands. But put an idiot in charge, some churl, and he'll pick off his own people as well."

"During the revolution, our nation nurtured its remarkable military leaders and was proud of them. It was they who cooled the combative ardor of the German and other fascists. But over the past few years, this pride of our nation has been physically annihilated."

And he would flex his old man's fingers on his hand as he called out the heroic names: Tukhachevsky, Yakir, Kork, Eideman, Blyukher... there weren't enough fingers. He waved his hand and made a prophetic pronouncement:

"Remember, Leonid Fedorovich! When the war starts — and it's not far off — the German armies will immediately capture half of Russia. Everything's been

---

[24] Feodor Vasilyevich Tokarev (1871-1968) was a well-known designer of Soviet small arms, including the TT (Tula-Tokarev) semiautomatic pistol and the SVT-40 semiautomatic rifle.

prepared for that. All of military art is a science. If you've only a priest's education, you can't teach this fine art to others, as is being done now. War is not the same as christening babies."

He did not utter the name of the person he was talking about. It was evident. That person's toadies exalted his military genius in every possible way, calling him "the supreme military commander of all times and peoples." We had no shortage of ode composers.

I well remembered the predictions of dear old Feodor Vasilyevich. So when the war began on June 22, 1941, and Stalin was soon designated the People's Military Commissar and Commander-in-Chief, I immediately bolted from Moscow to the East, away from the fascists, as it was absolutely obvious what was in store for the country if its armed forces were to be led not by a military leader but by a man with a priest's education. I knew, from my own experience, that war was, indeed, not the same as christening children. Feodor Vasilyevich was right, and he was a true Russian patriot.

To be on the safe side, I took with me a small trunk of photographic materials (of which there was a shortage at that time in the country). I was supplied with the materials by a salesman from that same second-hand commission shop, to which I had delivered foreign records for a long time.

I ended up in Kazakhstan, in the South, a little closer to the sun. I had not even been able to sell my goods when I was grabbed and soon had 8 years of imprisonment stuck on me with another 3 years of restricted civil rights.

Leonid Fedorovich fell silent, thought for a while, and then ended his narrative.

"Yeah, they nailed me for a pinch of snuff. Before, I tossed thousands around right under the Kremlin's nose, and — nothing!"

* * *

December 1945. Winter. Snow. From a farm not far from the Chilik stream, one hundred sixty prisoners set out on foot through the deep snow after stacking felled lumber, up into the mountains to a spruce forest that appeared blue against the white snow background. Tied together with rope into groups of ten for safety, these people set out on goat paths to fell trees in the winter, so as to repeat their ordeal year after year.

Among these one hundred sixty people was Leonid Fedorovich Dubrovskiy, the man with whom I had become friends, and whom I had grown to be quite fond of despite his shortcomings. Will we ever meet again? I was departing on a special detail in the opposite direction.

February 1970

Captain Ivanov's
Crime

I saw him the first time outside the zone. He seemed strange to me: stooped, thin, dressed in an English overcoat that was too short and did not fit, with rumpled captain's epaulets, wearing rubber shoes and a greasy protective cap with a red band. It was winter, and he, having pulled his head into the similarly well-handled collar of his overcoat, was running in small steps, mincing rubber.

Local camp officers were the complete opposite of the newcomer. They presented an immaculate appearance and conveyed a look of importance as they walked around the camp. They treated the mass of convicts with great indifference, and those above the rank of lieutenant didn't even take note of the "rabble."

These were jailers, as they were called by the convicts. As a rule, they were uneducated people and had no civilian specialty. For them, the jail and camp was the only place of existence. They distinguished themselves by their callousness and ignorance. From their many years of dealing with "kings" of thieves, they acquired not only their language, but also their outlook on life and their knack for easy pickings. Just like the *urki*, they passionately hated the "politicals" and "counterrevolutionaries." And their ardor was by no means the result of their patriotism. No, it was just that they knew that their various machinations would be condemned only by the "politicals."

Even among camp leadership, however, there were individuals who were distinguished by their humaneness and decency. These, although they were the same jailers, had some kind of civilian specialty, which served as a sort of an outlet "just in case," if they were suddenly to be kicked out of the security apparatus. Or they were army officers, often with high military rank, who had smelled gunpowder at the front and had ended up in the security apparatus by some inscrutable path. They, as a rule, took a closer look at the "cushy life" offered by the camp and soon quit the security apparatus for civilian life "of their own free will."

2

I worked as a divisional agronomist on a parcel of land. I lived inside the zone, in the central hall, and walked to work (our site was located 2 km from the center). The chief of the division was a very dear man, Stepan Nikitich Tkachev, a Ukrainian and a man with no military rank. He was kept as a chief because of his knowledge of local environmental conditions and of agriculture (which was the principal activity at this camp). He himself had been a local prosperous peasant who managed to reorient himself in time and even join that apparatus that could have, in due course, liquidated him as a class.

So once, he says to me:

"Did you know I'm quitting my job? I'm leaving for Ili, to the civilian life. They've already send someone to replace me."

"Who might that be?" I thought. "Not the captain?"

Soon, my guess was proved correct. The new divisional chief was captain Ivanov.

Already during our first face-to-face meeting he admitted that before the war, he had worked as a jail overseer and had never done anything in agriculture. He even expressed doubt as to whether he was capable of giving this camp division a go. I explained that, as the divisional agronomist, I in actuality managed the site's husbandry. I suggested that if he really had no knowledge of agriculture, that he take the time to become familiarized and to learn, and most important, not to get in my way. On this we entered into our spoken agreement. He shook my hand and began to hint to me of some upcoming large expropriation that we could hustle through together, as if I was some kind of robber. Meanwhile, he thought, one needed to properly get one's bearings. I understood him immediately and let him know that I was not a criminal, but a political prisoner, and would not embark on any "enterprises." The captain stopped short, became sour, and shut his mouth. Later, he began to complain to me of his misfortune. Having been demobilized with his wife from the army, he was returning from Hungary with a pile of various goodies. And, imagine, they got completely cleaned out in Kiev.

"What Marusya and I were wearing, we sold along the way. Now I haven't a penny to my name," he said.

Now it was clear why he had arrived at the camp in winter in an old overcoat and rubber shoes.

3

Work at the site continued in full swing. The captain really didn't understand anything about it. In the evening, in the office, he would simply sign papers, without understanding what they were for. He very much enjoyed checking and approving the work details for convict teams.

Team leader Kostin was a tough old bird, and he quickly took the measure of the captain. Every day, his team, which had previously lagged behind, began to perform 160%–180% of its daily assignment. He accomplished this very simply. At the start of the assignment, he wrote down the work actually done, which was perhaps 40%–50% of the daily allotment, while the rest was pure *tukhta*, as they called it in the camp. For example, you'd see the following work entries: "storage of smoke," "double transfer of same smoke," etc. All of this "work" was documented with appropriate numbers, including units of measure, the production standard, the total produced, and percentages. The glory of Kostin's team resounded throughout the camp. Former thieves and parasites had begun to demonstrate miracles of heroic labor. The idea of re-educating serious criminals had found its embodiment in the assiduous activities of captain Ivanov, and was expressed by his endorsing, every day and with his own signature, a report on the most recent *tukhta*.

The captain was happy; things were going well. The only thing that upset him was the absence of his family.

"Oh, how I miss my daughter and wife. I need to get them to the camp."

Marusya, the captain's wife, and their three-year-old daughter, lived 45 kilometers from the camp in a suburban state farm. Just like the captain, she hadn't a penny, so it fell to me to collect various old stuff in the division's storerooms, so as to bring the captain's wife and her daughter, hale and healthy, to our site via sleigh.

Once, I stopped by the captain's apartment. He was not home. But his wife, who was sprawled on a warm Russian oven, invited me from her supine position to sit down and wait for Lyonya (as she called her husband), who ought to be home any second. She was exceedingly garrulous, knew of my existence, apparently, from her husband, and immediately began to address me using the familiar form.

"Once spring arrives," she said, rolling her eyes, I'll find myself a young man..." and then primly added: "After all, what does a cat do when it has nothing to play with?"

With these words, the essence of Marusya became apparent.

4

Soon, Lyonya obtained a complete new regulation uniform, became happier, and tried to better understand the process of running the facility.

Spring was approaching. The ice on the river that blocked the road to Alma-Ata was about to break up, and thus, the distance to town would increase by about 50 kilometers owing to the detour over the Ili bridge. We needed to build our own bridge. The need to do so had become ever more apparent for some time, but there wasn't appropriate material available, and construction had been put off year after year. The new chief took up the fulfillment of this historic task. He first toured the vicinity on horseback, and then one fine day arranged for a pair of sleighs, took six career criminals from the zone and took off with them at night (he, on horseback; they, on sleighs) in some unknown direction. In the morning, at the crossing where the bridge was supposed to be built, there lay about a dozen railroad rails, which had been expropriated by the captain from the storage area of the neighboring railroad.

Construction of the bridge began in early spring, while there was still ice on the river. About 15 or so piles had to be driven into the bottom of the river. The piles were driven by convicts standing in the water. "Attending" to the health of the constructors, the captain drew several liters of alcohol from the storehouse. When the piles had been driven, a booze party got underway on the shore. However, most of the alcohol found its way not to those who had been in the water, but to those who had supervised the work: the captain and the guards who had stood watch over the convicts. That evening, the convicts returned to the central hall with stretchers carrying captain Ivanov and two soldiers, all of them roaring drunk, together with their weapons. The incident was truly extraordinary, but it was soon forgotten. The main thing was, none of the convicts had escaped.

Warm days were at hand, and the divisional chief prepared to deliver a report at a party meeting on preparations for spring sowing. It turned out that he couldn't even write down the required numbers in his notebook. I wrote a note, and even from that he barely could read. But he already had his trump card: he had mobilized internal reserves and built a bridge across the river.

Prior to the sowing, a shortage of horse harnesses was found. The captain, with the help of those same criminals, had cleaned out the stable of a neighboring collective farm. The captain's expropriators later were heard to boast of how easy it was to work with the captain:

"We bust the locks while he covers us on horseback with his pistol."

True, that most recent operation of the captain's turned out poorly. On the next day, trackers from the collective farm found their own harnesses in a stable storage room of the captain's division. They complained to the colonel, the camp commander, because the captain swore at them, saying that he knew nothing about any harnesses belonging to others. The colonel understood what was going on and gently said:

"Well, take them back. This business was caused by convicts and criminals. That's why they're in prison. We will re-educate them. But not all of them at once."

The listeners were satisfied with how the colonel had tiptoed around the issue, so they took their harnesses and set off homeward. And captain Ivanov managed to come up smelling like a rose once more.

5

By spring, captain Ivanov's younger brother Ivan had appeared at the parcel, excessively gangly, with an outward appearance very much like Lyonya's. I saw him as he loitered near the door of the colonel's office. Just prior to the departure of the tractor detachment into the field, the younger Ivanov was designated the detachment commander. He had never studied mechanics and had only seen tractors from a distance, but he did have a third-class chauffeur's license. Such a leader could introduce quite a hurly-burly into the work of the detachment.

But this did not happen. The detachment was staffed with experienced machine operators, including a mechanic, a foreman, and tractor drivers from among the convicts. The tractor drivers gave credit to their mechanic and foreman for their knowledge of the hardware, and it was possible that the new commander would invite catcalls. But surprisingly, the younger Ivanov immediately won the hearts of many tractor drivers. I could not understand what might have caused such affection.

It turned out that this Ivanov was a former recidivist thief. He was a small-timer, to be sure, who had served two short sentences by then, which was why he quickly found a common language with his people. He had promised the tractor drivers a pile of privileges that he was to obtain through his brother Lyonya, so that in the future, under his leadership, they were going to live big! The tractor drivers also learned something about his brother, the captain. The story of the elder Ivanov called forth a storm of emotions.

"He's one of us! That's the captain!" they would say, recounting his adventures to others.

6

The captain's past actually said quite a bit about him as a very busy individual. He had been a sergeant in the internal security troops before the war. Afterward, during the war, as a member of an interdiction detachment, he displayed miracles of bravery — in the rear, though, and against his own Soviet troops. He rose quickly as a result of this, and by the time our troops had crossed into Eastern Europe, the four small stars of a captain glittered on his epaulets. Special Section Captain Leonid Stepanovich Ivanov.

His unit was based in Hungary, and there he developed an insatiable appetite for illicit gain. First, to his amazement, he noted that Hungarians had a weakness for gold objects such as watches, wedding rings, earrings, and small crucifixes on chains, which were worn by very many quite ordinary people, whereupon he immediately carried on a struggle with this despicable metal and those fetters of capitalism. He organized night raids in apartments, returning to his quarters with the spoils of his searches.

All Hungarians detained for various reasons by patrols and who ended up at the special section in front of captain Ivanov left (if they left at all) relieved of exactly that amount of weight as their gold possessions weighed. Besides, he didn't take the watches in their entirety; he would break off their cases and then throw the rest away.

History has remained silent regarding the extent to which the captain undermined the faith of our potential allies in higher ideals. After all, gold items had often been bequeathed from grandmothers and grandfathers.

The situation in the country was gradually returning to normal, and Ivanov hurried. Soon, his stash amounted to about a kilogram and a half of scrap gold. But the captain was not exclusively interested in gold. He was not indifferent to "rags," as he himself scornfully referred to them. Marvelous material for suits and dresses, various ready-made clothes for both men and women, suits, coats, and dresses gradually were packed tightly into voluminous, solid leather trunks of English manufacture, which had been requisitioned from the bourgeoisie and which had marvelous locks that seemed to open and close at the sole whim of their new owner.

When control of the country was handed over to the Hungarians and our personnel began demobilizing, the captain urgently summoned his brother Ivan (who had recently completed a short prison sentence) from the USSR. Using some kind of fake document provided by the captain, the brother quickly appeared in Hungary. They drank to their meeting, and Lyonya quickly brought his brother up to speed.

"Understand, Vanya," the captain whispered, "this will set you and me up for life."

Soon, they came up with a plan for returning to their homeland.

7

While the captain and his wife were processing their demobilization, Ivan repaired a sedan abandoned by Germans. They wrapped the gold in rags and hid it in the spare tire after having first made a hole in the tire and then patching it. The spare looked like an ordinary tire, pumped full of air and not capable of arousing suspicion even if someone were to check it. The Ivanovs knew what fate awaited them if the gold were to be found. The expropriators anticipated everything. Having loaded the car with as many trunks as it could carry, they departed to the East. But our travelers immediately experienced bad luck. At the Soviet border, after the document check, they were told:

"Now, comrades, take your trunks out of your car and beat it over the bridge. Park your car over there on the side. Yesterday, we received an order that effective this morning, entry into the USSR in personal vehicles is prohibited. Only motorcycles are allowed.

The brothers were stunned. Ivan drove the car over to the side and they slowly made their way, bent over under the weight of the trunks, into the land of the Soviets.

8

In Kiev, captain Ivanov appealed to the personal representative of Beria, the USSR Minister of Internal Affairs, and was sent off to be at the disposal of the Ministry of Internal Affairs of the Kazakh SSR. From Kiev, his brother Ivan traveled to his mother's place somewhere near Moscow.

The captain and his wife did not want to check their trunks. "They'll be stripped, who knows?" they thought. "Those railroad workers are also wolves, and you don't dare put a finger in their mouth. They know where the gravy is. The route is long. Along the way, they'll leave assorted junk to make up the weight of items they steal. Then take it to court and prove anything!" So they decided to take all of their trunks with them and transport them in their compartment. Fortunately, there were only two sleeping berths in the whole compartment.

While waiting for the train to approach the platform, all of the trunks were piled on the platform of the Kiev Railroad Station. The brothers ran off to have a pleasant drink, leaving Marusya and her daughter with the things.

Soon, some rogues started a bloody fight behind Marusya. Marusya devoted all of her attention to the combatants. The police came at the run. As the last policeman was leaving the platform, leading away the disturbers of the peace, Marusya turned back to what she had been left to watch over. To her horror, the trunks had disappeared. In their place, several roguish sparrows were hopping around, picking up crumbs. Just at that moment, as through foreboding disaster, the brothers returned. Marusya started to make excuses, explaining what had happened.

"Shut your yap!" yelled the captain in his fury, and after directing every sort of invective at her, he fell over onto a bench as if shot.

Soon, the train arrived at the platform. The Ivanovs occupied their compartment light-handed. Along the way, they sold whatever knickknacks were in their possession and barely made it to Alma-Ata.

9

The spring of 1947 arrived slowly. The division's entire tractor detachment was already in the field and awaiting the command:

"Start your engines!"

The fields needed to be cultivated with Vlasenko thrashels as soon as possible, so as to trap moisture for fall-seeded crops and fall-plowed land. The tractor drivers were bored of having nothing to do, told each other various stories and tall tales, but didn't say anything out loud about their boredom. "What's it to us? The sentence get served even if you lie in your bunk."

Sometimes one tractor would be started and sent around a field on a tentative basis. But it would sink so deeply into the wet soil that harrows had to be put underneath to get it back out onto the road. It was still early. The soil had not matured.

Ivan Borovikov, the old tractor driver, who had somehow been left alone with me, told me:

"Watch out, agronomist, our new team leader will match you up with a second sentence. He's got greedy plans for the seed."

I had thought about the seed, and its safety, before this. Hundreds of quintals of select grain had been delivered to the fields for sowing. Meanwhile, the town was not far off, and seed was expensive and hard to find at the market. I felt that the Ivanov brothers were ready to avenge all their past failures in any way possible, and decided to speak with the captain regarding the safety of the seed during the sowing, relying on a number of newspaper articles on the subject.

I told him that if he and I messed up with the seeds during the first spring planting, everything would become known within a month. The seeds had been tested for viability, and if we don't put them in the ground, the only thing that would grow in the fields would be tall weeds. And if that happened, they wouldn't go after me, the agronomist, but him, the boss.

He agreed with my reasoning and I believe that all the seed intended for sowing was used as it should have been, in the ground. True, the head of the tractor detachment, apparently at his own initiative or in response to an inborn habit of stealing something if he could, tried to hide several bags of seed. But nothing came of it for him. The hidden bags were found, and the seed was planted. Some of the tractor drivers participated in my fight for the safekeeping of the seed. They understood that even camp fields was a branch where they lived fairly well in comparison with the convicts that worked in areas far removed from agriculture. Here, on the other hand, if you grind a head of grain, you can eat it.

Sowing came to an end in a workmanlike manner. The sprouts delighted the eye.

After sowing, preparations began for the haymaking, the next agricultural campaign. Semirechensk perennial blue alfalfa grew like it was leavened with yeast in fields used for fodder crop rotation. As the alfalfa fields were crossed with irrigation ditches, the hay harvest could only be done using horse-drawn haycutters.

Simple hay-harvesting machines were repaired in the parcel's smithy, and harness makers repaired the tack. It was just at that time when the captain overreached himself with the collective farm harnesses. But he had pursued that operation for the public good, for the common cause. It was true that, without their harnesses, the collective farm the captain had robbed might have found itself in a pickle. But this was beyond the captain's understanding, just as had happened in Hungary with the appropriation of other people's crucifixes.

10

Preparations for the next agricultural campaign were proceeding well. There was a problem, though, with the feed for the horses. All of the available raw grain stock in the bins had been, for some unknown reason, classified as an "emergency ration," and not a single kilogram could not be distributed without authorization from Alma-Ata.

We harnessed Percherons to the hay-harvesters. These were strong horses with a plodding gait that hauled the entire hay harvest every year. Hay was normally cut from early in the morning to late in the evening. The alfalfa had to be cured during its budding stage. If you're too late, you'll harvest either hay or fuel. But Percherons don't work well without meal for feed. I mentioned this several times to the captain; he in turn reported to the colonel and always got the same answer:

"Emergency ration." There is no feed.

Concerned for the success of the hay harvest, I appealed to the colonel myself. I explained that by the time we finish the hay harvest, barley (we had no oats) would ripen first in the fields, and then we could always replenish that amount of grain that we had taken from the "emergency ration." It was a win all the way around. The chief agreed with me, and soon I was carrying an order for two tons of barley. That very day, the grain was received from the central storehouse and poured into the crib of our division's stable, which was within the responsibility of the senior convict-stableman.

You can imagine my surprise when, the next morning, I arrived at the stable and saw that no grain had been given to the horses after they had been watered. Nor did I find a single grain in the stable's crib. When I asked the senior stableman what happened to the grain, he despairingly waved his hand in the direction of Alma-Ata.

From the stable, I immediately went to the captain's apartment (it was next door). Neither the captain nor Vanya were home. Marusya told me, as if nothing had happened, that they had left for town the previous night. Everything became clear. The grain had been taken to the market. This just about killed me. What was I to do? I had a long sentence, and you can't go anywhere, tied for long years to this juggernaut. You forgot your status as a slave when you worked at your business, and the days passed without notice from one agricultural campaign to the next. But now what?

Heartsick, I left for the field and there I met Mishchenko, the contract irrigation system manager. His position was subordinate to mine, and we often conversed about our business. He noticed my depressed state and immediately guessed what had caused it. He already knew about the grain. He lived next to Ivanov and saw all of the previous night's operation. Outraged, he said nothing to me but got on his horse and rode off to the central hall. There, he reported everything to the colonel.

The colonel, who had worked his entire life as an investigator, immediately translated all of the events into legal language. A staff was assembled regarding this incident, and it decided to set up an ambush at the bridge over which Ivanov had to cross when he returned from town. Exactly at midnight, Ivanov's carts drove up to the bridge. A search turned up empty grain bags and a pair of new leather coats, a black one with a baize lining, and a brown one, half of which was trimmed with fur.

The brothers had been caught with the goods. The next day, Ivan Ivanov, the chief of the tractor detachment, was fired, and the captain was dismissed from his position, since officers could only be assigned to and removed from work by the minister of the republic, with the advice of the camp commander.

11

One agricultural campaign was succeeded by the next. A bountiful harvest was poured into the silos, the stubble was ploughed, autumn wheat was sown, fall-plowed land was turned, and throughout, camp division No. 2 remained without a chief.

Once, upon meeting me by accident, the colonel told me:

"You know what? The Ivanov case is on hold. It turns out that dismissal from the security services is not something that can be decided by the local minister. The case has been referred to Moscow, to Beria[25]."

By the way, the colonel was so civil about this matter that over the course of the entire Ivanov episode with the grain, he never asked me anything about him.

Some more time passed. White flies began flying outside. Finally, the long-awaited answer arrived from Moscow, from Beria. To begin with, he pointed out the political nearsightedness of the Kazakhstan Minister of Internal Affairs, who had not immediately suppressed this mistreatment of captain Ivanov, a valued operative of the

---

[25] Lavrenty Beria (1899-1953), director of the Soviet secret police.

During World War II, as a member of the State Defense Committee, he played a major role in raw-materials production using the slave labour in the camps.

Soon after Stalin's death in March 1953, Beria became one of four deputy prime ministers and apparently attempted to use his position as chief of the secret police to succeed Stalin as sole dictator. By July 1953, however, he was arrested, deprived of his government and party posts, and publicly accused of being an "imperialist agent" and of conducting "criminal antiparty and antistate activities." Convicted of these charges at his trial in December 1953, Beria was immediately executed.

security apparatus. Colonel Mazyukov, who had formalized the "case" against Ivanov, was to be dismissed from the security services. And an order was given to immediately return captain Ivanov to his previous position, and to pay him for the time of his enforced absence.

12

Ivanov was out of his mind with happiness. He demanded that I be immediately removed from the division, even though he knew, from the case file, that I had not participated in his downfall.

I was escorted under guard to the central zone and locked. Major Bunin, who had been sent to replace the colonel, called me into his office and spent a half hour didactically beating the idea into my head that workers of the Ministry of Internal Affairs were the foundation of our state, Party, and comrade Stalin. Any doubts regarding their revolutionary honesty was a crime, as they have stood and continue to stand on guard for those revolutionary gains that have been made against the numerous enemies of Soviet power, etc., etc. Then he began to list all of the trials, from the Shakhty and Promparty trials to those against various enemies of the people, etc.

I kept quiet. Many years of penal servitude lay before me. I had a family. I wanted to live.

The major, having exhausted his eloquence, fell silent. Then, as if declaring an end to the discussion, he told me:

"I will nevertheless use you in your specialty. You may go."

13

Soon, I was assigned to the first camp division, located about five kilometers from the central hall, *as a tally clerk.* The major did not fulfill his promise to use me in my specialty, but I did receive a pass that enabled me to move about without an escort guard.

Nevertheless, you could expect anything at all from Lyonya. He would have liked to pin some kind of sabotage on me at the division (it was fashionable, then), but he could not find allies, nor did he have the intelligence to fabricate something. I heard through the grapevine that Ivanov had even avenged himself against the horse I used to ride by driving it out, and that it had died.

One day, I came to learn some completely secret news from certain sympathetic fellows from the records and assignment section of the camp: a prisoner transport was to be sent to Mongolia to construct a railroad. The first group to go had been selected on the basis of health, and at the insistence of captain Ivanov, I and my friend G. N. Vladislavlev, also a political convict, had been included in this prisoner transport, although the state of our health should have never allowed us to be included in the first group. He also knew that he was to leave with this transport. In making his farewells, he said to me:

"Mind you, the departure is scheduled for tomorrow."

Evening was approaching. I was supposed to spend the night in the division zone and, consequently, to hand in my pass at the guard post. I couldn't sleep all night. Recently, my wife and four small children had moved several thousand kilometers in order to live closer to me. Now, if they commandeer me to Mongolia, will I ever see them again? I tossed and turned in my bed, then got up and went outside. It was still the middle of the night. I dozed off before dawn and when I woke up, it was gray outside. I quickly dressed and went to the guard post. "Is there a pass there? Will the guard let me by?" questions such as these ran through my head.

The young guard promptly found my pass and gave it to me.

"Well, Lyonya, now go chase the wind in the field!" I said to myself, and in the darkness, I set off into the field, to the highest point, from where I could see the entire central hall and camp division No. 1 (to which I was now assigned), as if they were in the palm of my hand. There, I lay down in a dry irrigation ditch and having covered myself with wild grass, began to observe.

When the time came to split up into teams for work, no split occurred. And apparently, none would occur, as preparations were being made for the departing prisoner transport. Then a pair of soldiers rode from the office of the central hall. "This," I thought, "is for me." They hung out at the division for about an hour and a half, and left to return empty-handed. "A fig to you!" I sent that thought their way from where I was. Finally, people began to be led with their things from the central zone. "The transportees," I calculated. "Georgiy Nikolaevich, apparently, is with them." They were counted for a long time, formed into a column, and finally loaded onto trucks and driven away in the direction of the railroad.

A couple of hours after the prisoner transport departed from the central hall, a pair of new horsemen appeared and headed again to my division. Their horses were lively. "The top brass," I guessed. They rode by not far from where I was. They were the above-mentioned major Bunin and authorized operative junior lieutenant Sonin.

"Well," I thought, "now I can announce myself."

I rose to my full height and also headed toward the division. The assistant troop commander caught sight of me from afar. He rode up to me on a foamy horse, apparently having traveled extensively in his search for me.

"Where were you?" he yelled.

I quietly answered that I had been at work, but that I had experienced an attack of malaria (I really did suffer from malaria), and I had lain for several hours in the field. I told the same story to the top brass. They suspected something, but legally they couldn't pin an attempted escape on me. But they did take away my pass, transferred me to the central hall, and assigned me to heavy earthmoving work.

14

The days passed. I continued to work doing heavy earthmoving. It so happened that I ran across the camp's senior mechanic at the strip pit, a contract engineer named Grigoriy Nikolaevich Berezhniy, with whom I had worked a couple of agricultural seasons. He took a look at me and my pick, shook his head, and then bent down from his horse and quietly said to me:

"Don't worry. Tomorrow, I'll go to Alma-Ata and talk about you with the very top man in the administration, Cheremisyn."

Then he looked off toward the central hall and said, through clenched lips: "Rabble and thieves!"

Then he turned to me and whispered: "Wait for news." And he rode away.

The third day after my conversation with Berezhniy was a day off, a Sunday. A guard appeared at the threshold of the barracks where I lived and loudly pronounced my name.

"Report to the guard post with your things!" he concluded.

Initially, I came out without any things at all. But the same guard explained that I needed to report with my *personal* belongings, and not to take along my bedding.

That meant I was going to be taken somewhere. Strange, that it would happen on a day off. But there was no time for discussions. I said my farewells to Feodor Semenovich Yudin, my neighbor, with whom I had been able, over a short time, to form a strong friendship, and set off for the guard post.

Along the way, I kept wondering: "Where? To whom?" I only knew that I would not end up with the prisoner transport headed for Mongolia.

There was a passenger car near the gates, and next to it was a man of the rank of captain. He politely explained to me that he was the commander of the Ili camp, that he was in need of an agronomist, and that at the recommendation of G. N. Berezhniy, he had arranged for the camp administration to detail me to his camp.

Indicating his portfolio, he said:

"All of the paperwork has been completed. Please take a seat." he spoke to me using the formal second person and indicated the seat. "And we'll be off."

A new camp life began for me. What new things will it bring me?

Prior to my imprisonment, all representatives of the agencies of coercion appeared to me to be a rude, close-knit group not only in their mode of dress, which united them, but also in their common inner substance, the same way, for example, that we today imagine members of Ivan the Terrible's *oprichnina.* But now, after three years of imprisonment, I became convinced with my own eyes, that no such *commonality* exists among them.

Once, when I was alone with a young lieutenant who was the chief of the cultural and educational detachment, he said to me:

"I actually envy you and would trade places with you with pleasure."

The feeling of sympathy for convicted innocents, apparently, never abandoned people, no matter what clothing they wore. To my surprise, among the officers tasked with enforcing the law, I met those who deeply sympathized with me.

The question of where I would end up, with friends or not, could not but worry me.

January 1970

Information of the Department of the Committee for State Security,
Republic of Kazakhstan, for the Eastern Kazakhstan Oblast:

Sokolenko, Aleksandr Konstantinovich
Born in 1907, educated in the humanities; Ukrainian, school teacher.
Place of residence: E. Kazakhstan Oblast, Aksuatsk District, Aksuat village.
Arrested July 25, 1944 by the People's Commissariat of State Security.
Sentenced: Semipalatinsk Oblast Court, November 15, 1944, guilty of
violating article 58–10 of the RSFSR Criminal Code.
Sentence: 7 years in a labor camp.

Exonerated on September 15, 1956, by the USSR Supreme Soviet
for lack of any element essential to the crime.

TABLE OF CONTENTS